Anonymous

Proceedings of the

Reunion of the First Iowa Cavalry

Anonymous

Proceedings of the
Reunion of the First Iowa Cavalry

ISBN/EAN: 9783337733629

Printed in Europe, USA, Canada, Australia, Japan

Cover: Foto ©ninafisch / pixelio.de

More available books at **www.hansebooks.com**

PROCEEDINGS

OF THE

FIRST REUNION

OF THE

FIRST IOWA CAVALRY.

HELD AT

Davenport, September 19, 20, and 21, 1883

HISTORICAL SKETCH

BY SURGEON M. B. COCHRAN.

DAVENPORT:
EGBERT, FIDLAR, & CHAMBERS.
1884.

FIRST REUNION

FIRST IOWA CAVALRY.

In February, 1883, D. A. Kerr commenced corresponding with members of the First Iowa Cavalry, having in view the holding of a reunion of the regiment the following autumn; and, at the reunion of the Iowa Veterans' Association, held in Des Moines on the fifth day of April, all the members of the regiment there present were invited to meet in the Aborn House for consultation in regard to the matter.

The result of that meeting will be seen in the following circular, which was issued and sent to every member of the regiment whose address could be obtained:

"FIRST IOWA CAVALRY REUNION.

"*To Comrades of the First Iowa Cavalry Volunteers:*

"At a called meeting of as many of the members of the First Iowa Cavalry as could be reached, held at Des Moines, Iowa, April 5th, 1883, David A. Kerr was elected Chairman, and Geo. M. Walker chosen Secretary. After a full discussion of the question under consideration, which showed a most favorable feeling toward holding a reunion, on the motion of Geo. M. Walker, the following preamble and resolutions were unanimously adopted:

"WHEREAS, Letters have been received from a very large number of the ex-members of the First Iowa Cavalry, all expressing an earnest enthusiasm and anxious desire that the surviving members of the First Iowa Cavalry should hold a reunion, and promising to attend wherever located ;

" 1. *Resolved*, That it is the earnest wish and desire of this representative body of the ex-members of the First Iowa Cavalry, that a regimental reunion should be held during the fall of 1883.

" 2. That the location of said reunion and time of holding the same be referred to an executive committee with power to act accordingly.

" 3. That the following comrades are hereby appointed said executive committee :

"DAVID A. KERR, Keokuk, Iowa.
"JAMES HILL, Keokuk, Iowa.
" WM. GOODIN, Farmington, Iowa.
" M. B. COCHRAN, Davenport, Iowa.
" E. J. BABCOCK, Davenport, Iowa.
" L. E. DEAN, Lyons, Iowa.

" Now, therefore, in compliance with the spirit of the above resolutions, and regarding the preferences expressed by a majority of the members heard from, the Executive Committee have decided to locate the reunion at Davenport, Iowa, September 19th, 20th, and 21st, 1883, (same date as the Eastern Iowa Veteran Association Reunion), and we most cordially invite all who were ever members of the First Iowa Cavalry to meet in a grand reunion for fraternal greeting, and to unite in the breaking of 'hard tack.'

" Arrangements have been made with the railroads and steamboat lines for transportation on the most favorable terms, and with the hotels for accommodations at reduced rates.

" All ex-members of the First Iowa Cavalry are most urgently requested to aid the Executive Committee by corresponding with and urging each other to attend the reunion, and in securing the names, (company), and present post-office address of all who were members of the regiment, and forward the names to David A. Kerr, Keokuk, Iowa.

" For any further information desired in regard to the reunion please address either of the following parties: E. J. Babcock, Secretary, Davenport, Iowa; M. B. Cochran, Davenport, Iowa, or L. E. Dean, Lyons, Iowa.

> " Fraternally Yours,
>> " DAVID A. KERR, *Chairman,*
>> " E. J. BABCOCK, *Secretary,*
>> " L. E. DEAN, *Treasurer,*
>> " M. B. COCHRAN,
>> " JAMES HILL,
>> " WM. GOODIN,
>>> " *Executive Committee.*"

Early in August, Circular No. 2 was issued and sent to every member (about 700) whom the committee could locate, and, in a large number of cases, personal letters were sent by some member of the committee, urging the comrades to attend the reunion.

> " FIRST IOWA CAVALRY REUNION,
>> DAVENPORT, IOWA,
> September 19th, 20th, and 21st, 1883. }

" *To Comrades of First Iowa Cavalry Volunteers:*

" Arrangements have been made for reduced rates of transportation for comrades and their wives who attend the reunion at Davenport, Iowa, September 19th, 20th, and 21st, 1883, with the following railways:

> " Chicago, Rock Island & Pacific.
> " Chicago, Milwaukee & St. Paul.
> " Chicago, Burlington & Quincy.
> " Chicago & Northwestern.
> " Central Iowa Railway.
> " Burlington, Cedar Rapids & Northern.
> " Des Moines & Fort Dodge.
> " Sioux City & Pacific.
> " St. Louis, Keokuk & Northern.
> " Chicago, Burlington & Kansas City.
> " Rock Island & Peoria.

" Reduced rates over the Chicago & Northwestern are *via* Clinton, De Witt, and Wheatland; the Central of Iowa, *via* Grinnell. The other roads from any station on their lines.

" Rates of fare over the above-named roads are one full fare coming and one-third fare returning. Orders for return tickets will be furnished by the Secretary to all members and their wives who attend the reunion. The Illinois Central Railway declines to make any reduction in their rates.

" Arrangements have been made with the different hotels to accommodate all who come, at from $1.25 to $2.00 per day.

" From the numerous letters received from comrades, by the Executive Committee, it is a settled fact that this will be the largest reunion of any regiment ever held in the State of Iowa.

" The Eastern Iowa Veteran Association hold their reunion here at the same time. That includes the old soldiers of the Second Congressional District. They number over 2,000, and will go into camp for the three days, in regular army style. Drills, parades, and sham battles, with artillery, infantry, and cavalry, will be the order of the day. We are cordially invited to participate in their reunion. Any of our regiment who wish to go into camp with them, are invited to do so. Tents and rations will be furnished.

" This joint reunion will be the largest ever held in the State, except the one at Des Moines, in 1870. A committee, wearing First Iowa Cavalry badge, will be at the depots on arrival of trains, to direct comrades to Armory Hall and hotels. Everything that it is possible to do is being done by the Executive Committee to make this first reunion of the regiment a perfect success. Every member of the regiment is earnestly requested to answer to roll-call September 19th to 21st. Let every one decide at once that he will fall into line, and exert himself to see that every member that he has any knowledge of, reports promptly for duty. Every one that can do so, is requested to notify the Secretary, not later than September 1st, of the fact that they will unite with us in the breaking of ' hard tack.'

" Fraternally Yours,

" E. J. BABCOCK,

" Secretary Executive Committee."

"DAVENPORT, IOWA, June 29, 1883.
" E. J. BABCOCK, ESQ.,
"*Secretary Committee on Reunion First Iowa Cavalry:*

"*Dear Sir:*— We, the undersigned Committee of Arrangements for the reunion of the Eastern Iowa Veteran Association, respectfully invite the First Iowa Cavalry to participate with us in a reunion, to be held at Davenport, September 19th, 20th, and 21st, 1883.

"H. EGBERT, *Chairman,*
"J. B. MORGAN, *Secretary.*"

The Eastern Iowa Veteran Association arranged to hold their reunion, which had been located in Davenport the year previous, on the same days in September, and invited the First Cavalry to unite with them in all joint exercises; which invitation was thankfully accepted by the Executive Committee.

On the morning of September 19th the Executive Committee met in the parlors of the Kimball House and arranged the programme for the public exercises of the reunion as follows:

WEDNESDAY, SEPTEMBER 19.

7:30 P. M., Reception at Burtis Opera House.

THURSDAY.

Forenoon, Meeting of Regiment at Armory Hall. Afternoon, Street Parade with Eastern Iowa Veteran Association.

FRIDAY.

Forenoon, Excursion to Rock Island Arsenal. Afternoon, Sham Battle at the Fair Grounds, by Eastern Iowa Veteran Association and Co. B, I. N. G.

At 7 P. M. the Opera House was filled by members of the regiment and Veteran Association, and ladies and gentlemen of Davenport, Rock Island, and vicinity.

Col. Henry Egbert, Chairman of the Executive Committee of August Wentz Post, G. A. R., presided.

On the stage were Ex-Gov. Kirkwood, Hon. H. R. Claussen, J. P. Van Patten, E. S. Carl, Maj. Geo. P. McClelland, Surgeon C. H. Lathrop, Capt. Aug. Reimers, Gen. Add. H. Sanders, Maj. C. H. Toll, Capt. R. M. Reynolds, Chaplain Rand, Prof. Kramer and the Harmonic Chorus, and the members of the Executive Committee of the First Iowa Cavalry.

In the audience were Col. D. W. Flagler, of Rock Island Arsenal, Gens. W. W. Belknap, Wm. Vandeveer, and other distinguished veterans. After a splendid overture by Strasser's orchestra, Chaplain Rand, of the First Iowa Cavalry, offered prayer, after which the orchestra rendered a number of inspiring martial airs which called forth hearty applause.

This was followed by an address of welcome by Hon. H. R. Claussen, Mayor of Davenport, and as he stepped forward and the veterans caught sight of the G. A. R. badge upon his breast they gave him a most enthusiastic greeting. He said that on behalf of the city of Davenport, as its present Mayor, it was his pleasant duty to welcome the First Iowa Cavalry to our midst and to extend to them the freedom of the city; "not that words should be at all necessary to assure you of the most affectionate welcome of our patriotic citizens. The soldier's badge you wear is the surest and best passport to the gratitude and to the esteem of our people." The Mayor then alluded to the opening of the war, and said the proud name they bear, the "First" of Iowa Cavalry is well calculated to stir up old recollections. He alluded to the calls of "our great and glorious War Governor, Samuel J. Kirkwood," and at the mention of the name, the audience broke into tumultuous and prolonged applause. He then depicted the responses to these calls, and so spoke of the condition of the State, with no superfluous population to spare, and of her contributions to the armies of the Republic. He then spoke of the distinctive features of the First Cavalry's service — of the manner in which they made their services known and felt in the field, and of their maintenance of the honor of the State and the cause of the Nation. He alluded to the visit of the Villard party of capitalists to the Northern Pacific Railway they have built, and of the honors accorded them, and said "that after all, the thought comes home to us, that to the citizen-soldiery of America the very possibility of these accomplishments is due, for a united country only could, and a united country only would, build these great works of civilization." After refering to the lesson America gave the world, in the result of the war, the Mayor concluded with again welcoming the regiment to the city.

The Harmonie male chorus then sang "Tenting on the Old Camp Ground," accompanied by Prof. Cramer at the piano. The selection, which was rendered with unusual effect and was received warmly, was followed by the introduction of R. M. Reynolds, of Washington, D. C., Captain Company A, First Iowa Cavalry, who spoke at some length. Capt. Reynolds confessed that no words of his could even begin to convey the grateful pleasure it gave him to see his old comrades received in Davenport by such a magnificent assembly. Capt. Reynolds then extended hearty thanks to Mayor Claussen and the populace of Davenport, for their hearty reception. He spoke of the First Cavalry, and this, the first gathering of the regiment since the time, now twenty-two years ago, when the First Cavalry gained its immortal reputation, gained by being the "first in and the last out;" when they were summoned and responded to the second call by President Lincoln, for forty thousand volunteers; when, too, the Second, Third, Fourth, Fifth, Sixth, and Seventh Iowa — and the other Iowa regiments, until the list becomes too long for enumeration — responded at the first appeal for men. Capt. Reynolds referred to the changes and surprises of the past twenty-five years, and stated that the hearty reception thus given by Davenport to the First Iowa Cavalry, and the many other veterans present at the great reunion, was to him not the least pleasant surprise, and made evident the fact that there are none but loyal hearts in Davenport. He then again thanked the Mayor and citizens for the magnificent reception. When Capt. Reynolds closed his remarks, which were received with storms of applause, the male chorus sang in the best of form, the inspiriting strains of the patriotic "Rally 'Round the Flag."

Dr. M. B. Cochran was next introduced, and read his "Historical Sketch of the First Cavalry."

HISTORY OF THE FIRST IOWA CAVALRY.

Under a proclamation issued May 3d, 1861, the President of the United States called into service of the government 42,034 volunteers to serve for three years, unless sooner discharged, to

2

be mustered into service as infantry and cavalry, and by General Order No. 15 (1861), the proportion designated by the war department was thirty-nine regiments of infantry and one of cavalry.

Prior to that time the nucleus of several cavalry companies had been formed in different parts of Iowa. A company was organized in Iowa City early in April, which developed into Company F, and another at Clinton that grew into Company B. These several companies, ten in all, were tendered to the President by Governor Kirkwood as an independent regiment of cavalry, and it was one of the first, if not *the* first, cavalry regiments offered to, or accepted by the President.

On the 13th of June, 1861, the captains of these several companies received notice from the Governor to hold their companies in readiness for further orders, and on July 18th ten companies received orders to proceed to Burlington for muster into United States service. This order embraced the companies from A to K. At that time ten companies was the requisite number for a regiment of cavalry. Within a few days, however, the number of companies for a cavalry regiment was increased to twelve, and Companies L and M were subsequently added to the regiment.

COMPANY A

Was organized in Keokuk, and most of the men were residents of Lee county. The company had had a temporary organization for some time prior to the receipt of the Governor's order of July 18th, and on the evening of the 24th they met at the court-house for permanent organization. W. M. G. Torrence was chosen captain, A. G. McQueen first lieutenant, and R. M. Reynolds second lieutenant. The company mustered ninety-five men, rank and file, most of them between the ages of twenty-four and thirty years.

On Saturday, the 27th, the citizens of Keokuk turned out to bid the company good-bye. The City Rifles, under Capt. W. W. Belknap, and the Keokuk Cavalry, under Cap. Sample, as escort, marched up to the corner of Main and Fourth streets, where Company A was in line. On behalf of the ladies of Keokuk, Hon. Samuel F. Miller presented a flag to the company, on receiving which Capt. Torrence replied: "We thank the ladies for this beautiful flag, and we will defend it to the last, and when it shall be trailed in the dust my wife will be a widow and my children orphans."

Comrades of Company A, behold your old flag, borne gallantly for five long years of war, its stars undimmed, its stripes still bright; and though he in whose hands it was placed, and many of the brave boys who stood beside him that July morning, gave their lives for the cause they loved so well, and sleep the soldier's last sleep, that emblem of liberty was never lowered in the presence of an enemy. Its guardians kept it well.

As we look back over twenty-two years, the forms of that gallant band stand before us as they appeared that day. We see the quivering lips, and mark the struggle to keep back the tears that tell of feelings too deep for utterance, and as the good-byes are whispered by lips that do not dare to trust the open voice, and hands are pressed, perhaps for the last time on earth we again realize the price that was paid for the liberty, peace, and prosperity which we now enjoy.

Escorted by the City Rifles and Sample's Cavalry, the line of march was down Main street to Second, and then out on the Montrose road, to Burlington. They camped that night at Denmark, where they remained over Sunday, and on Monday morning reached Burlington.

COMPANY B

Was a development of the "Hawkeye Rangers," organized in Clinton, some time before the war. The company was raised mostly in Clinton county. Its first captain was W. E. Leffingwell, than whom a braver or more gallant officer never wore the uniform of the service. S. S. Burdett was first and William De Freest second lieutenant. Many of the men of Company B were inured to camp life, from their occupation as lumbermen, and for physical strength, firmness, and endurance, they excelled any company in the regiment. Not one was rejected by the mustering officer, and throughout their term of service they were always ready for business.

COMPANY C

Was enlisted in Burlington and its vicinity. Major W. E. Chamberlain was largely interested in raising the company, and he was indefatigable in his efforts to get the regiment into quarters. It was largely made up of men of from eighteen to twenty-five years old—some of them of very boyish appearance, but plucky and true as steel.

On the final organization of the company, Levi Chase was chosen captain, and Benjamin Ranney and A. F. Dean first and second lieutenants.

COMPANY D

Was recruited in the counties of Warren and Madison. P. Gad. Bryan was chosen captain, and J. D. Jenks and William Shriver were first and second lieutenants. The men were all young and of splendid physique, always ready for duty, full of pluck and good nature, and were never out of rations.

Capt. Bryan was successively promoted to major and lieutenant-colonel of the regiment, the latter of which he resigned in 1863. Lieutenant Jenks was an elder in the Presbyterian church, and was cross-eyed, two conditions, when combined in the same man, will ensure the best material for an officer. He was afterwards promoted to major, and brevetted lieutenant-colonel of volunteers for gallantry at Dardanelles, Arkansas.

COMPANY E

Was recruited in Henry county. William Thompson was chosen captain, and W. P. McClure and T. A. Bereman were first and second lieutenants. Captain Thompson was afterwards promoted to major, and then colonel, of the regiment.

Lieutenant McClure was compelled to resign, in 1862, on account of severe disease of the eyes. Lieutenant Bereman resigned in September, 1862, but was called back to the captaincy of the company on promotion of Captain Thompson. He was promoted to major in 1865, and served to the final muster-out of the regiment.

Such officers could not fail to enlist an excellent class of recruits, and such were the men of Company E.

COMPANY F.

On the 28th of March, 1861, a meeting was held in Mendenhall's hall, Iowa City, to take measures to organize a company of cavalry. The meeting adjourned to the 15th of April, when another meeting was held in Market hall. Thirty-five names were enrolled, and an organization was completed. J. O. Gower was chosen captain, J. W. Porter first lieutenant, John Borland second lieutenant, and J. R. Elliott orderly sergeant.

The company met for drill regularly from that time until it was ordered into quarters by the Governor. Some of the original members left the company, and many other names were added to the roll, and a reorganization was effected before final muster into the United States service. J. R. Elliott was chosen first lieutenant, P. E. Shaver second lieutenant, and C. E. Dustin orderly sergeant.

The company reached Burlington on the 29th of July, 1861.

COMPANY G

Was raised in Hardin, Dubuque, Blackhawk, Jones, and Delaware counties. In April, 1861, a company was raised in Hardin county for the Sixth Iowa Infantry, of which J. D. Thompson and E. S. Foster were members. After the fall of Fort Sumter these gentlemen withdrew from the Sixth, and began recruiting a company of cavalry. A meeting was held at Eldora, and it was there decided to raise and mount a company of cavalry, to be known as the Hardin Rangers, and tender their services to the government. J. D. Thompson was elected captain, J. Edgington and L. E. Campbell first and second lieutenants, and E. S. Foster orderly sergeant. There was no trouble in securing men, but it was not so easy to procure horses. Each man had to furnish his own horse, and, as many of the men were not able to do this, a large number recruited for the Rangers, left the company and joined the infantry.

The nucleus of a company had been formed in Dubuque by H. H. Heath, and Captain Thompson proceeded to that place to arrange for a consolidation, which resulted in the organization of Company G, with J. D. Thompson as captain, H. H. Heath as first lieutenant, L. E. Campbell as second lieutenant, and J. M.

Simeral orderly sergeant. About that time a call was made for
a regiment of cavalry from Iowa. Information was received
from Washington that the government would furnish horses to
all who could not supply themselves, and the company was
rapidly filled. They moved to Burlington via Ottumwa, and at
Eddyville, joined Company H.

Lieutenant Campbell did not respond when the order came to
move, and E. S. Foster, was chosen second lieutenant, on arriv-
ing at Burlington.

COMPANY H

Was largely recruited in Monroe county, by Captain Dan.
Anderson and Wm. Whisenand, who brought a detachment
from Lucas county. On the organization of the company Dan.
Anderson was chosen captain, and Riley Westcott and William
Whisenand first and second lieutenants, and A. U. McCormack
orderly sergeant. As this was the first company raised in that
part of the state, it was composed of choice men. All the pro-
fessions, and nearly every industry in the state, was represented
in it, and it is sufficient to say that every man, in his military
history, not only honored his profession, but his regiment, his
state, and his country.

Captain Anderson was successively promoted to the rank of
major, lieutenant colonel, and colonel, and Lieutenant Whisenand was promoted to the rank of major, and Lieutenant Westcott and Sergeant McCormack succeeded to the captaincy of
the company.

COMPANY I

Was enrolled in the counties of Wapello and Keokuk, and recruited by Captain J. W. Caldwell and Lieutenants D. C. Dinsmore and W. H. Kitterman. On the third of May, 1861,
Captain Caldwell began recruiting a company, to be in readiness
when the call should come for more troops. He was a Virginian
by birth, and had an appreciation of the magnitude of the
rebellion and the determination of the foe we had to meet. He
had a heart, every pulsation of which beat with loyalty to the
Union — as brave as a lion, and as tender as a woman — the
soul of honor and patriotic manhood. He was a man of splendid physique, a fine horseman, and exceedingly fond of sorghum.

Company I was a body of men fit for such a leader to command, and they never failed to come to time, when needed.

COMPANY K

Was enrolled in the county of Clayton, and recruited by Captain R. L. Freeman, Dr. Thos. H. Barnes, and Lieutenant A. L. Freeman. Captain Freeman was a soldier in the Mexican war, and in those days a military record of any kind was worth a commission and a company of men, to the possessor of it. Captain Freeman was an excellent officer, and brought into the regiment some of its best material, and his men were never ashamed to have it known that they belonged to Company K. Their efforts to relieve the monotony of camp life were untiring and eminently successful. It was a couple of men from Company K who *surrounded* a house one night near Osceola, captured eleven of the enemy, disarmed them, and took them into camp next morning.

By an act of congress approved July 29th, 1861, regiments of cavalry were increased to twelve companies instead of ten, and as soon as this information reached Burlington steps were taken to add two additional companies to the First Cavalry.

Lieutenant H. H. Heath and Sergeant J. M. Simeral of Company G, and Sergeant D. C. McIntyre of Company B, were authorized to recruit Company L. As fast as recruits were sent in they were mustered into service, and about the last of September Lieutenant Heath brought in the main body of the company, which was duly organized by the choice of H. H. Heath, captain, and D. C. McIntyre and James M. Simeral first and second lieutenants. The men were mostly enrolled in the counties of Dubuque, Jackson, and Jones, and mustered ninety-four, rank and file.

Company L contained the only man of the First Iowa who ever confessed to running from the enemy in a fair fight, and in his case he claimed "mitigating circumstances." He had been a member of Company I of the First Infantry, which fact alone will condone any reasonable military dereliction. It was at the battle of Wilson's Creek, and from behind the cover of a friendly log, he was doing his best to put an end to the war, when a man with a sword came up and ordered him to "get out of that — that's an officer's log." He said he didn't exactly run, but hurried back to take a new position.

COMPANY M

Was composed, in part, of the men who could not get into Company B. Many of them claimed that they were enlisted for the First Cavalry, but as the complement of ten companies had already been assigned to the First Cavalry, when they were ready to go into camp they were ordered to rendezvous at Davenport with the Second Cavalry. As soon, however, as the order was received increasing the number of companies for a cavalry regiment to twelve, measures were taken which resulted in taking Company M from Davenport to Burlington, completing the organization of the First, with twelve full companies, numbering 1,052 men, rank and file.

Fitz Henry Warren was appointed colonel; Chas. E. Moss, of Keokuk, lieutenant colonel; E. W. Chamberlain, of Burlington, and Captain J. O. Gower, of Company F, majors; M. B. Cochran, Company F, surgeon; D. B. Allen, Indianola, assistant surgeon; M. L. Morris, of Company F, quartermaster; H. L. Dashiel, Company H, commissary; D. A Kerr, Company A, J. M. Bryan, Company D, T. S. Edsall, Company B, adjutants; John A. Landis, Company I, C. A. Case, Company M, W. H. Muzzy, Company K, battalion quartermasters; Jas. W. Latham, chaplain.

Col. Warren, at the time of his appointment, was the army correspondent of the New York *Tribune*. He was in Washington at the time the first Bull Run battle occurred. He wrote a series of articles for the *Tribune*, under the caption "On to Richmond," in which he sharply criticised the early prosecution of the war. His letters did not suit those in authority, and he received instructions from the managers of the *Tribune* to modify their tone, and some of them were changed by the editor before publication. This caused him to sever his connection with the *Tribune*, and determined him to enter the military service. He was a man of keen intellect, very impulsive, warm in his friendships, and bitter in his enmities — "independent in all things, and neutral in nothing," and one who, if he did not harmonize with his superiors, was an exceedingly uncomfortable man to have around. He was proud of his regiment, and his assignment to the command of the First Cavalry was hailed by officers and men with unbounded joy.

Lieutenant-Colonel Moss had been a soldier in the Mexican war, and that fact gave him prestige that few in the regiment possessed. He was a man of great kindness of heart, brave almost to recklessness, and zealous in the discharge of every duty.

We had been but a few days in camp when an order was received to proceed to Keokuk, in anticipation of a rebel raid from the Missouri border. Although we had no arms or military equipment of any kind, the enemy was not aware of tha fact, and the presence of a thousand mounted cavalry without arms, at that time had a formidable appearance, and our presence was all that was necessary. We remained in Keokuk four or five days, and then returned to camp in Burlington.

Early in October, 1861, the regiment was ordered to St. Louis, and as soon as transportation could be procured we proceeded by boat to that point and went into quarters at Benton Barracks. Before the entire regiment reached St. Louis, Companies A, B, F, and G were ordered to Jefferson City, to report to General Pope. They went by boat up the Missouri river, joined Pope, and accompanied him to Springfield, where they remained until Fremont was relieved by General Hunter.

Concerning that march to Springfield and return, I have these notes from a member of Company B : "I remember that while in Benton Barracks, in the fall of 1861, we were told that Fremont was fitting out an expedition to go after Price, Shelby, and Marmaduke, and other rebs, and that shortly after Company B, and, I think, F, were detailed to act as body-guard to General Pope on the expedition. Our march to Springfield was slow and tedious, with many stops. We were surrounded constantly by bushwhackers, and it was dangerous to get out of sight of the command, and yet I remember that chickens, eggs, etc., were plentiful with Company B, and that we had some to spare always for General Pope's mess. Of course he knew

3

nothing about it, and would not eat chicken, as there was an order forbidding foraging off the country.

"As we neared Springfield, the command was threatened on all sides, as the enemy had massed their forces there and showed fight. We did not unsaddle our horses for three days, and finally went into the city on a run, as the enemy left it at the same pace. Price marched his command about thirty miles south, into the Cross Timbers.

"Fremont had an army of western men—eager, compact, cool, and determined, and he was their *beau ideal* of a soldier. They urged him to let them go and 'lick Price out of his boots.' He promised them they should do it in a few days. Then an order came removing Fremont and putting Hunter in his place. The whole army cried and swore. Hunter came — the army that Fremont and his noble wife had almost created by the lavish use of their energy and money was disbanded and scattered in the face of the enemy, and we returned to the Missouri river. Price followed us and held the south part of the state for several months." Such were the impressions made on the mind of a young soldier at that time, and they have not been erased.

Companies C and H were soon after ordered to Jefferson City, and remained there under Major Gower, scouting and on garrison duty during the winter of 1861-2.

About the 1st of November Companies D and I were ordered to Tipton, Missouri, and joined the First Battalion on their return from Springfield, and in the meantime Captain Torrence was promoted to major.

In December, Companies A, B, D, F, G, and I accompanied General Pope on an expedition to western Missouri, and on the return, the First Iowa, First Missouri, and two companies of the Fourth Regular Cavalry, under command of General Jeff. C. Davis, captured about 1,300 recruits for the Confederate army, under command of ex-Governor McGoffin. About one thousand stand of arms, with all the camp equipage of the command, were taken. This was the first capture of any magnitude made in Missouri, and the first victory of General Pope. It was almost bloodless, for the enemy were surprised just after they had gone into camp. We made a double-quick march of nearly twelve miles, ran in their pickets, and had them corralled in the bend of Black river before they suspected any danger.

On the return of the command, the First Iowa went into camp at Georgetown, and remained there until near the close of 1861.

On the 8th of January, 1862, Companies A, F, G, and I, with a detachment of the First Missouri Cavalry, attacked and completely routed a rebel camp of recruits under Colonel Poindexter at Silver Creek, Missouri, marching over two hundred miles between the 3d and 8th. In that engagement we lost our first man in battle — James Convey, of Company F — as brave a boy as ever lived. He was but a boy in years, but every inch a hero. I found him on the field a few minutes after he was shot, and saw that, in all probability, the wound would prove fatal in a few hours. He was also conscious that he had answered to roll-call for the last time, and said to me: "Well, some lives must be sacrificed in this cause, and it had far better be mine than one with wife and children dependent upon him." Brave words, bravely uttered, and worthy to be written in letters of living light.

After this engagement the detachment returned to camp at Georgetown and remained there until February. In the meantime, Companies B and D were sent to Lexington, and were kept busy scouting the country in that neighborhood. While stationed at this point, word was brought to camp one day that a slave who had escaped from his master before Mulligan's surrender of Lexington, entered the Federal lines, and had been of marked service to Mulligan, and was recaptured by the Confederates and sent back to his master, was a chained prisoner in his master's house near Lexington. Lieutenant Jenks, with a party of men of Company D, went out to the plantation to learn the facts. The master of the slave denied there being such a man on the plantation, but while the conversation was going on Lieutenant Jenks heard the clanking of chains. He insisted on searching the house, and found in one of the chambers a stalwart negro with a chain riveted upon him, the length of which was about twelve feet, and the links made of iron nearly three-quarters of an inch in diameter. They took him to a blacksmith shop and had the rivets cut and the man set free. The chain is now in the rooms of the State Historical Society in Iowa City. The slave went to Kansas and enlisted in the first of the negro regiments raised in that state.

During the month of February Companies A, F, G, and I, with two companies of the Eighth Iowa Infantry, all under command of Colonel Geddis, made a successful raid to Warsaw, Missouri, a distance of fifty miles, capturing several officers of the confederate army, among whom was General Tom Price. The march of fifty miles and back was made within thirty-six hours.

The remainder of the winter of 1861-2 the four companies, A, F, G, and I, were scouting along the Missouri Pacific railroad; Companies B and D at Lexington, and Companies C and H at Jefferson City on similar duty, while Companies E, K, L, and M remained at St. Louis under command of Colonel Warren.

In March, 1862, Colonel Warren was ordered to establish his headquarters at some point in western Missouri, southwest of Sedalia, so as to guard the western part of the state and cut off supplies that were constantly being sent to Price's army in the south; and during the latter part of that month all the companies of the regiment were brought to Sedalia, and on the 8th of April, headquarters were fixed at Butler, Bates county, and detachments stationed at Osceola and Clinton. On the 13th, a scouting party, composed of Companies D and K, under command of Lieutenant-Colonel Moss, were attacked by a party of guerrillas at Montevallo, and after a fierce engagement, the enemy was repulsed with a loss of two killed and several wounded, and a number of prisoners and horses captured. Our loss was: Oscar Crumb and James Whitford, of Company K, killed, and three wounded.

On the 2d of May Colonel Warren, with two hundred men and Section F, First Missouri Artillery, marched to the Marie des Cygnes and captured thirty prisoners and a quantity of powder and lead found buried.

On the 15th of May the forage train from Butler was attacked by bushwhackers, and J. H. Bird and Andrew Forst, Company D, and Martin Merideth, Company E, were killed, and one man wounded; and on the 26th, Dexter Stephens, of Company I, was killed by guerrillas. On the 27th a forage train from Osceola was fired upon, and W. G. Harbach killed, and Josiah Cameron and Michael Higgins mortally wounded — all of Company C.

On the 8th of June a detachment of one hundred men under command of Lieutenant Reynolds, of Company A, went from Clinton to Cass county, and discovered a band of about two hundred guerrillas, under command of Quantrell, on the Lotspeach farm. Finding them too strongly posted in the timber, after a loss of one killed and two wounded, he withdrew. On the 9th all the serviceable men of Companies A, G, H, and M, with a small body of the First Missouri Cavalry, all under command of Major J. O. Gower, struck the trail of Quantrell's band four miles west of Pleasant Hill, in Cass county, and soon found them well posted in the timber cliffs of Big Creek. Major Gower attacked them with great energy, and after a spirited contest, completely routed them, killing and wounding a large number. In this action the First Iowa had three men killed: Snell Dodge and James Beecroft, of Company G, and G. W. Collins, of A, and ten wounded, among whom were Lieutenants Reynolds and Foster, and Adjutant Kerr, the latter severely.

On the 3d of May Major Torrence resigned to accept the Lieutenant-Coloneley of the Thirtieth Infantry, and ill-health compelled the resignation of Lieutenant-Colonel Moss. Captain Bryan was promoted to major, and on the 10th of July to lieutenant-colonel.

It was about this time that an incident occurred which showed quite clearly the odor in which the Union soldiers were held by the women of the south. A lieutenant, of fine personal appearance and gracious manners, and possessed of the gallantry that particularly distinguished the officers of the First Cavalry, being out one day on a foraging expedition, stopped at a farmhouse, and was met at the door by the proprietor, who invited him inside and entertained him most hospitably, introducing him to his wife and two daughters. The owner was courteous, the ladies were gracious, and after partaking of an excellent dinner, and spending an hour or more in delightful conversation carried on largely between the young ladies and himself, he took his departure, promising himself to return again some other day when forage teams went out that way, which resolution was strengthened by the cordial invitation of the proprietor to call whenever he passed in that direction.

He had not been long in camp when an old darkie came in, and recognizing the lieutenant, he made himself known as the slave of the gentleman with whom he had dined. In the conversation which followed, the lieutenant spoke of his master's daughters in a complimentary manner, when the old contraband replied: "Yes, mas'r, deys's fine ladies, but dey's mighty bad secesh, do; and dey hates de Yankees powerful." "Why," said he, "they were very pleasant to us, and treated us very kindly." "Yes, but you doan know what dey did arter you'ns was gone." "Why, what did they do?" "Why, dey burnt rags over de house."

On the 2d of August a detachment from Companies E, L, and M, under Captain Caldwell, encountered a band of three or four hundred guerrillas in the timber on Clear Creek, in St. Clair county. The outlaws were well armed, and under command of the notorious Clowers. After a brief but desperate struggle, in which the enemy lost eleven killed, our troops, being greatly outnumbered, withdrew to the prairie to await reinforcements. In the meantime the enemy retreated out of reach, and no further action took place. Our loss was four killed and twelve wounded, among whom was Captain Heath.

The posts at Butler and Osceola were now broken up, and the Regiment returned to Clinton, and for the first time after leaving Burlington, all the companies were united again. Soon after Colonel Warren received an order to take a large part of his force and join General Blunt, at Lone Jack, in pursuit of the rebel, Coffee, who had recruited a force in northwestern Missouri, and was crossing our line to go south. The united force gave chase, but did not succeed in overtaking them, and returned to camp after a march of over three hundred miles. The enemy was in sight nearly all the time. Our men suffered greatly on this march for want of provisions, and for three days had nothing to eat but green corn and fresh beef. It was while returning from this march that some of the men found a patch of watermelons, and securing a few nice ones brought them into camp. Colonel Warren, completely worn out with the fatigue of the march, spread his blankets in an ambulance after supper, and was soon asleep. When it became dark enough for "foraging" some of the men, who did not get any watermelon, started out "to see what they could see." Among them was Hospital Steward, Ed. Winters, a man of an inquiring mind and great perseverance when looking for commissary stores, but a constant martyr to his own mistakes.

He came to the rear of the ambulance, not knowing that it was occupied, and quietly letting down the tail-board, saw something round and white, and sure that he was right this time, he seized the colonel's bald head. Now, the colonel was not the most amiable man in the world when he was tired, still less so when wakened from a sound sleep, and much less so when awakened in that particular manner. The explosion that followed brought out the guard, who thought the mules were all loose. Winters had no idea that anything in war was so frightful. As soon as he could catch his breath he told the Colonel it was all a mistake on his part, and that he was very sorry. He thought his head was a watermelon. That was as far as he ever got with his apology; the fire was too heavy for him, and he "lit out" for the hospital.

Early in September Colonel Warren resigned to accept a commission as brigadier-general. Lieutenant-Colonel Gower was promoted to colonel, Major Bryan to lieutenant-colonel, and Captain Caldwell to major, and on the 20th the regiment broke camp at Clinton and took up the line of march to Springfield, Missouri, and for the first time was assigned to a brigade.

The service of the regiment, up to this time, had been of the most distasteful character — hunting guerillas and bushwhackers. To be wounded or killed where contending forces meet in a fair field and with fair warning, amid the roar of artillery, the rattle of musketry, and clashing of sabres, may be glorified by a vivid imagination, into something grand and heroic, but to be maimed or shot to death by a cowardly bullet from the brush, can neither be painted nor sung so as to possess one element of either grandeur or heroism, and it was a matter of rejoicing when it was known in our regiment that we were to become a part of the "Army of the Frontier." Colonel Dye, of the Twentieth Iowa, was our brigade commander, and we were assigned to the third division. From Springfield we marched through Jollification to Newtonia, and from Newtonia through Gadfly to Cassville, and on the 18th of October crossed the Pea Ridge battle-ground at Elk Horn Tavern, and camped on Sugar creek, near Bentonsville, Arkansas.

On the 20th, at five P. M., we broke camp and marched all night, and next day "stood to horse" on White river.

On the 22d we marched all night to near Huntsville, then back to camp; next day to Mud Town and back; from thence to Cross Hollows, to camp at Valley Springs.

On the 27th ten companies left camp at nine P. M., marched all night and surprised a camp of the enemy at Magruder's crossing, captured their breakfast, camp equipage, and a few prisoners, and drove them into the Boston mountains.

That day our quartermaster, S. C. Dickenson, one of the most faithful officers of the regiment, was killed by guerillas while out with a foraging party near Cross Hollows.

The next day the ten companies returned to camp, where the regiment remained until the 4th of November, when an order came to return to Missouri. We returned over the same road by which we entered Arkansas, as far as Cassville, and then, by way of Ozark, marched to the old battle-ground of Wilson's Creek, where we went into camp on the 22d. On the 25th, all of the available force of the First Iowa went on a scout to Yellville, Arkansas, returning on the 30th, having marched over two hundred miles.

The foregoing is a description of the kind and amount of work performed by the regiment during the summer and fall of 1862.

The "Army of the Frontier" was composed of three divisions — the first under command of General Blunt, the second under General Totten, and the third, to which the First was attached, under General Herron. General Totten, having obtained leave of absence as soon as the second and third divisions reached Wilson's Creek, the command of both divisions devolved upon General Herron.

On the morning of the 3d of December a dispatch was received from General Blunt, who was at Cave Hill, Arkansas, saying that he was threatened by a large force of the enemy under General Hindman. Within three hours the third division was on the march, and reached Elkhorn tavern on the evening of the 5th, There another dispatch was received from Blunt, requesting all the cavalry to be sent forward at once. The First Iowa, Tenth Illinois, Sixth, Seventh, and Eighth Missouri, and the second battalion of the Second Wisconsin Cavalry, were sent forward at once, all under command of Colonel Wickersham, of the Tenth Illinois, and reached General Blunt on the 6th at midnight, having been eighteen consecutive hours in the saddle.

The next day was fought the battle of Prairie Grove, in which the First Iowa participated. During the fight a few of the First Iowa recaptured a howitzer lost by the Tenth Illinois.

On the 27th, all of the available men of the regiment accompanied the expedition to Van Buren, Arkansas, and took part in the capture of that place and of five large steamboats loaded with quartermaster's and commissary stores for the enemy, and on the 31st returned to camp at Prairie Grove.

This closed the year 1862. The year 1863 opened with an order for the Third division to countermarch to Missouri again; taking a circuitous route in the direction of St. Louis, and on the 2d of January the First Iowa, under command of Lieutenant-Colonel Anderson, took the advance to scour the country along the flanks of the line of march, passing through Fayetteville, Huntsville, Carrollton, and Forsyth.

On the 10th, Major Caldwell, with about four hundred men, surprised and captured seventy-five guards in charge of extensive saltpetre works on Buffalo river. The works, with several tons of saltpetre, were destroyed. On the return Captain McQueen destroyed works of a similar character about ten miles from the former, and captured a drove of horses and mules destined for the Confederate service.

The campaign being now ended, and no immediate prospect

4

of further active service, Lieutenant-Colonel Bryan, Major Chamberlain, Chaplain Latham, Captain Westcott, Lieutenants Bishop and Freeman, and Adjutant Kerr (the latter being permanently disabled by a wound in the right arm received at Pleasant Hill, Missouri), tendered their resignations and were honorably discharged from service — thus depriving the regiment of many of its best officers. Captains Chase and Thompson were promoted to majors. Assistant-Surgeon Allen, one of the most accomplished medical officers, and a genial gentleman, resigned to accept a commission as surgeon of the Thirtieth Infantry. Sergeant C. S. Alber, of Company A, was commissioned quartermaster, John A. Ladd, assistant surgeon, and other promotions were made in the line.

The Third division moved from Forsyth to Lake Springs, near Rolla, and here, for the first time, the First Iowa was fully armed. Up to this time the men had been armed with every conceivable weapon, "from a Springfield musket to a pocket pistol," and though urgent requisitions had been made for arms, the government had been unable, until then, to supply them. They now received revolvers, sabres, and Sharp's carbines, and procured a fresh supply of horses.

On the 20th of April about six hundred of the regiment, under Major Caldwell, were sent out to meet General Marmaduke's raid into southeastern Missouri. A night attack was planned, and the First Iowa designated to execute it. The enemy was completely surprised and routed. Our loss was five men wounded.

The regiment returned the 15th of May, having marched over five hundred miles, and having suffered greatly from want of provisions and clothing.

About this time the "Army of the Frontier" was broken up, General Herron taking all the infantry and artillery to join the investing forces of Vicksburg. A division of cavalry was formed under command of Brigadier-General Davidson, to which the First Iowa was assigned.

General Steele was at this time organizing a force to penetrate the heart of Arkansas, making Little Rock the objective point, and General Davidson was ordered to join him with his cavalry on White river, above Helena.

Then commenced that terrible march through the swamps of southeastern Missouri and Arkansas, from which more men were permanently disabled by sickness than by any other exposure during the war. Miles of corduroy bridges had to be built, and the baggage was reduced to the smallest amount possible — and here the men first learned the use of " dog tents."

A junction was formed with Steele's forces at Clarendon, where they crossed White river, and they soon after engaged in the battle of Bayou Metaire, in which the First Cavalry took the leading part. This engagement resulted in the capture of Little Rock, which became the base of operations for the Union forces from that time.

In all the engagements which resulted in the capture of Little Rock the First Cavalry was in the advance continually. General Steele reported his entire loss of killed, wounded, and missing at less than one hundred, and of this number the loss of the First Cavalry was thirty-seven.

The remainder of the year 1863 was spent in the vicinity of Little Rock, and no event transpired worthy of special note. The men were badly used up by the march and exposure in reaching that place, and from the resulting sickness there were thirty-five deaths during the fall and early winter months.

Early in January, 1864, re-enlisting of the regiment, under the act of congress for enlisting " veteran " soldiers, was commenced, and before the end of the month more than one-half of the First Cavalry had re-enlisted for three years or during the war. They were then entitled to a furlough of thirty days, but as General Steele was fitting out an expedition to unite with General Banks on Red river, the veterans waived their right to return home at that time, and joined the Seventh corps in the Camden campaign.

Owing to a great scarcity of forage, many of the horses had died during the winter, and as a remount could not be obtained in that country, nearly four hundred of the men had to march on foot.

They left Little Rock on the 22d of March, Lieutenant-

Colonel Caldwell commanding a brigade, and Captain Crosby commanding the regiment. They were much of the time in the advance, and on the 30th had an engagement at Spoonville. On the 2d of April they met twenty-seven hundred of the enemy at Antoine, and had a running fight for five miles. On the 4th they encountered the forces of General Price at the Little Missouri river, and completely routed them. In this engagement the regiment lost thirty-nine men killed and wounded.

From this point to Prairie de Anne the First Cavalry had the advance, and were the first to enter the works at that place, holding the enemy in check on the right until General Steele passed with his main force on towards Camden.

On the 15th the mounted men of the regiment were again ordered to the front, and engaged the enemy at 7 A. M. After an engagement of six hours the dismounted men were brought up and deployed as skirmishers, pushing the enemy on through Camden.

The army going into camp at Camden, the veterans of the First Iowa, five hundred and twenty strong, were relieved from further duty and ordered to Iowa on thirty days furlough, and having sold their horses to the government, started on foot for Little Rock.

The day before they left Camden, a train of two hundred and forty wagons, under escort of the Second brigade, Third division, of the Seventh corps, left Camden for Pine Bluffs to procure supplies, and on the third day afterwards they were attacked by General Fagan with a force of eight thousand cavalry and two batteries of artillery, near Mark's Mills, on Saline river — and although Colonel Drake (commanding the brigade) stated in his report that they were "not whipped," a large number were killed or wounded, and the remainder captured.

The First Iowa veterans, in light marching order, reached a bridge across Moro creek a few hours after Colonel Drake's command had crossed it. This creek was narrow and deep, and could only be crossed on the bridge. The veterans could hear the noise of the engagement in front of them, and were pushing on rapidly to take a hand in it when it suddenly ceased. Only Lieutenant Nugen, of Company E, had crossed the bridge, and he was at once taken in by Confederate flankers, who undertook to cross the bridge to the west side. They were fired on by the veterans, and made a rapid retreat, taking Lieutenant Nugen with them. The veterans held the bridge until dark, and then fell back to join the forces of General Steele, which had evacuated Camden and were falling back on Little Rock on the Jenkins' Ferry road. They reached the command of General Steele, and participated with it in the battle of Jenkins' Ferry on the 30th, and with the Seventh corps returned to Little Rock, where the non-veterans and new recruits remained, while the veterans left on the 3d of May for Iowa, reaching Davenport on the 17th. They stopped, on the way up the river, at St. Louis, and presented to their old division commander, Brigadier-General Davidson, a most elegant cavalry sabre, which they had ordered made especially for him some months before.

At the expiration of their furlough, the regiment again assembled in Davenport, and on the 20th started for Little Rock. Before leaving Davenport, Colonel Anderson, Major Chase, Adjutant Donnell, Quartermaster Albers, and Commissary Da-hiell resigned, and Major Thompson was commissioned colonel; Captains McDermott and Jenks, majors; Sergeant Morrell, of Company A, adjutant; W. W. Fluke, of Company E, quartermaster; R. F. Newell, of Company I, commissary; Assistant-Surgeon C. H. Lathrop, surgeon, vice M. B. Cochran, appointed assistant-surgeon U. S. Volunteers; Hospital-Steward James Hervey, assistant-surgeon.

When the veterans arrived at Cairo they were ordered back to St. Louis to be remounted and equipped for the field. As soon as horses could be procured they were sent on a scout west of St. Louis, and afterwards stationed at points along the Northern Missouri railroad, where they were kept on patrol duty until the 1st of October.

On the 27th of September six men of the regiment, acting as guard for a number of prisoners on a railroad train, were stopped by the notorious outlaw, Bill Anderson, at Centralia. They were ordered out of the car and disarmed, and, prisoners and guard, about thirty in all, formed in line, and all shot to death. It was one of the most cowardly and brutal acts of the war. Major McDermott got on the trail of Anderson and followed it about two weeks, but could not overtake him. It is a satisfaction to know, however, that he was killed, with most of his band, not long after.

About that time Price commenced his last raid into Missouri. The veterans were ordered to Jefferson City and assigned to duty at General Rosecrans' headquarters, and participated in all the marches in pursuit of Price.

After the Missouri campaign was ended they procured fresh horses and equipments, and proceeded to join the other portion of the regiment at Little Rock. The original members of the regiment who did not re-enlist had been discharged, and the veterans and recruits of 1864, numbering in all nearly six hundred, mounted, harmonious and jubilant, entered upon the year 1865 ready for any duty or emergency which they might be called upon to meet.

Lieutenant-Colonel Caldwell having served the full time for which he originally entered the service, was mustered out in September. Major McQueen was promoted to lieutenant-colonel, and Colonel Thompson having been assigned to the command of a brigade, Colonel McQueen was left in command of the regiment.

On January 14th a detachment was sent, under Major Jenks, to Dardanelles to attack the Confederate Colonel Cooper with a force of sixteen hundred men. The enemy was routed, with a loss of ninety killed and wounded. For his gallantry in this affair Major Jenks was brevetted lieutenant-colonel of volunteers.

On the 22d of January the regiment, under Major McDermott, formed a part of the force of General Carr, and again marched to Camden, captured many prisoners and drove the enemy from that place. Company F, under Captain Dow, led the advance on this march, and particularly distinguished themselves for gallantry.

Returning to Pine Bluffs, the regiment received orders to proceed to Memphis, Tennessee, to operate against the rebel General Forrest, who with his band of guerrillas was committing depredations in that vicinity. They reached Memphis on the

2d of February, and on March 4th were a part of the command under General Shanks on his expedition to Grenada, Mississippi, and while at Ripley Colonel McQueen had an encounter with a part of Forrest's command on the Tallahatchie, defeating them after a brisk engagement.

The regiment returned to Memphis, and on the 3d of April, with all the available cavalry, they started on a tour through West Tennessee, and encamped at Colliersville, where they constructed comfortable cantonments, and made that point their base of operations until the final surrender of the confederate armies.

The war was now over, and the men were joyful in anticipation of soon being mustered out of service and joining their loved ones at home.

While hopefully indulging these anticipations, an order was received from Lieutenant-General Grant directing them to proceed to Texas. The disappointment was great, but on the 15th of June, with the Fifth and Twelfth Illinois, Second Wisconsin, and Seventh Indiana regiments of cavalry, they embarked on transports for Alexandria, Louisiana, reporting to General Custar on the 23d. Before the regiment was fairly in camp, special order No. 2 was issued, which will never be forgoten by any man of that command. August 7th general order No. 15 was issued.

I do not wish to uncover the grave of the dead to recount the events that occurred between the periods of the arrival of troops at Alexandria, and their arrival at Austin on the 4th of November, but justice to one of the most gallant regiments that was in the service compels me to say that no greater indignity was offered to any body of men during the war, than the issuing and attempting to enforce orders No. 2 and 15, and no greater proof of thorough military discipline and subordination was shown during the war than the submission to those orders, simply because they were issued by the chief officer of the command.

Let us exercise the greatest charity, and simply call it a mistake. If it was the first one of he who issued them, we should not judge him too harshly, and if he felt it and did not confess it, we must remember that it often requires more courage to confess a mistake than to face an enemy on the field of battle.

The regiment left Alexandria on the 8th of August, and reached Hempstead, Texas, on the 29th. Their rations were exhausted, many of the soldiers were barefoot, destitute of clothing and blankets, and their sufferings were infinitely worse than at any time during the war.

The regiment remained at Hempstead until October 29th, when they were ordered to Austin, at which point they arrived on the 4th of November, and where they remained until the 15th day of February, when an order was received to muster the men out of service. They left Austin on the 19th, and arrived in Davenport on the 13th of March, and on the 16th were discharged, paid off, and left for their homes, after an absence of nearly five years.

The total number of men enlisting in the First Iowa Cavalry, rank and file, was 2,187 ; of this number there were killed, 13 ; died during the war, 215 ; discharged for disability, 204 ; transferred to Veteran Reserve Corps, 14 ; transferred for promotion, 25 ; dismissed, 3 ; missing, 2 ; captured, 23 ; leaving 1,647 who were either mustered out at expiration of three years, or at the close of the war. Of the former officers and men of the regiment we have the address of 749. They are scattered over the country, in twenty-nine states and territories.

Of the original field officers of the regiment all have died, except Lieutenant-Colonel Moss. Lieutenant-Colonel Caldwell is also dead. Major Torrence, as colonel of the Thirtieth Infantry, was killed in battle at Cherokee Station, Alabama, October 21st, 1863.

Since the close of the war the only effort to get the regiment together was at Des Moines at the grand state reunion in 1870. So far as I can learn no effort was made to effect a regimental organization at that time. At the reunion of the Eastern Iowa Veteran Association, held at Clinton in 1879, the members of the First Iowa had a room set apart to their own use, and quite a number of the regiment met there, and it is said that an association was formed, but I have been unable to find any record of it.

Of the one thousand six hundred and forty-seven men honorably mustered out of service, we have been able to find less than one-half, and from this time on our roll-call will rapidly grow smaller and smaller. One by one our ranks are lessened by transfer to the "invalid corps" and final "muster-out." We enlist no new recruits. "We know no countenance on which is the sunshine of youth; we hear no voices fresh with the morning's melody; our noon-time is past; we are in the midst of the afternoon. The upturned faces on the battle-field were those dewy with youth; we remember them, as on them shone the early light — ours is the lengthening shadow."

"The mimic camp-fires that we build have in them no suggestion that our country's day will ever again be dark by the smoke of battle, where her sons shall contend with each other in mortal strife. They rather serve to light the pipe of everlasting peace, by kindling afresh in the mind the ever glorious fact that the people love liberty better than ease, and their country better than life."

"We have seen the generation that would stand where we stood twenty years ago, should the call to arms be sounded; we may safely trust their valor, and confide in their patriotism. Let us deliver to them the castle keys — we may sleep without fear."

However remotely we may be separated, soon final "taps" will reach the ear of all. May it be but the prelude of a reveille that shall waken us to a glorious immortality, where peace shall reign forever.

At the end of the Historical Sketch, in which Dr. Cochran was frequently interrupted by applause and out-spoken words from the audience, Col. Egbert introduced Gov. Kirkwood,

THE OLD WAR GOVERNOR,

the very mention of whose name brought forth such a thunder of applause that it was nearly five minutes before the house could again be quieted sufficiently for him to be heard. The Governor spoke as follows:

"GENTLEMEN OF THE FIRST IOWA CAVALRY: — This is your meeting. You want to shake hands with each other, and

5

recall the scenes and memories of the days when you were comrades, side by side, not listen to me. I have heard with great interest the reading of many of the reminiscences of your career, and the great war, by your historian. We have histories of the war and labored chronicles of the stormy times, written by ambitious Macauleys, but have no account of actual affairs in camp and in the field. What we want to know is what you were doing in camp. [Applause and laughter.] Take large sheets of paper — the 'legal cap' of the lawyers — and write these for us from your own personal reminiscences. Write them out, so that we can know what kind of men you were, on duty and off duty. We know how you fought, but what we want to know is what else you did." [Applause.]

At the close of Governor Kirkwood's brief, but peculiarly effective, remarks, Col. Egbert introduced

EX-SECRETARY OF WAR, BELKNAP,

who was also welcomed with uproarious applause. He spoke at considerable length, referring glowingly to the achievements of the First Cavalry, the pleasant occasion of this reunion, and urging as many as possible of those present to attend the reunion of the Fifteenth Iowa, shortly to be held at Cedar Rapids. After ex-Secretary Belknap's speech, Strasser's orchestra rendered a most beautiful and sympathetic selection, which was loudly applauded.

D. A. Kerr, who was Second Adjutant of the First Cavalry, was introduced, and spoke briefly, closing by urging the members of the brigade to meet at 8 A. M., sharp, to-morrow, at Armory Hall.

The Harmonic male chorus, lead by Professor Kramer, then sang, in incomparable voice and style, Kinkel's beautiful "Soldier's Farewell," and the meeting adjourned to 8 A. M., Thursday morning.

HEADQUARTERS FIRST IOWA CAVALRY, }
ARMORY HALL,
DAVENPORT, September 20th, 1883. }

The regiment was called to order by David A. Kerr. On motion of E. J. Babcock, E. S. Foster was elected Chairman, and P. H. Francis was elected Secretary.

On motion, a committee of one from each company was appointed to present articles for a permanent organization of the regiment. Nominations were made by companies, and resulted in the choice of the following named comrades: D. A. Kerr, A; E. J. Smith, B; C. M. Turner, C; Geo. M. Walker, D; E. T. Patterson, E; P. E. Shafer, F; John McDermott, G; W. S. Whisenond, H; E. C. Dinsmore, I; John Fitzsimmons, K; L. B. Manwaring, L; W. H. Rigby, M.

After consultation, the committee presented the following articles as a plan for permanent organization:

First. The name of the organization shall be, "The First Iowa Cavalry Association."

Second. The objects of this association shall be to perpetuate the memory and achievements of the members of the First Iowa Cavalry, to preserve that unanimity of loyal sentiment, and that kind and cordial feeling which has been an eminent characteristic of this regiment. The history and glory of the officers and soldiers belonging to this regiment, who have fallen, either on the field of battle or otherwise in the line of their duty, shall be a permanent and sacred trust to this association, and every effort shall be made to collect and preserve the proper memorials of their services, and also to complete a roster of the surviving members of this regiment, with a record of their present place of residence.

Third. The officers of this association shall consist of a President, First Vice-President, Second Vice-President, Secretary, and Treasurer, who shall be chosen by ballot, and hold their offices for three years, or until their successors are elected.

Fourth. There shall be an Executive Committee of twelve, composed of one member chosen by and from each company, and who shall hold their offices for three years, or until their successors are chosen from said companies. The officers of this association shall be *ex-officio* members of the Executive Committee, and the President of this association shall be chairman of said committee. Any nine members thereof shall constitute a quorum for the transaction of business.

Fifth. All who were ever members of the First Iowa Cavalry, and who were honorably discharged from the service, shall be eligible to membership in this association, by complying with the requirements thereof.

Sixth. All persons eligible to membership in this association shall be admitted therein by giving their names, rank, company, and post-office address, and paying an admission fee of one dollar, and tri-annual dues of one dollar.

DUTIES OF OFFICERS.

First. The President shall have power to call a meeting of the Executive Committee whenever he may choose to do so, and he shall call a meeting of the Executive Committee on the written request of a majority of all the members of said committee; he shall preside at all meetings of the Executive Committee, and of the association, and he shall issue all orders made on the Treasurer.

Second. The Vice-Presidents shall perform all duties devolving on the President, in his absence.

Third. The Secretary shall receive all moneys due the association, giving his receipt therefor, and pay them over to the Treasurer, taking his receipt for the same; he shall countersign all orders drawn by the President on the Treasurer, and keep a correct record of all the proceedings of the association, and of the Executive Committee, and turn over all papers and books of his office to his successor, when duly elected.

Fourth. The Treasurer shall receive all moneys from the Secretary, giving his receipt therefor, keep a correct account of the same, and pay them out on the order of the President, countersigned by the Secretary.

Fifth. It shall be the duty of each member of the Executive Committee to hunt up and keep a record of all the members of the company which he represents, and ascertain their post-office addresses, and all facts pertaining to their personal history, so far as their military record is concerned, or anything pertaining thereto. The Second Vice-President shall perform the same duties for the members of the commissioned and non-commissioned field and staff, and forward all such information to the Secretary. The Executive Committee, when called together, shall have power to transact any business, in the interest of the association, which may be brought before it, and they shall have power to call a reunion of the association every three years, at such time and place as a majority of them may agree upon. They shall also have power to fill any vacancy in their own body that may occur by reason of death or resignation of any member, such vacancy being filled by a member of the same company as that to which the member so dying or resigning belonged.

Sixth. These articles may be altered or amended at any meeting of the association, by a majority vote, notice of the same being given one day previous to the vote on such alteration or amendment being taken.

The articles were amended, so as to make the bond of the Treasurer $1,000, to be approved by the Executive Committee, and, as amended, were unanimously adopted.

The following named comrades were then elected officers of the association for three years:

DAVID A. KERR, President.
H. S. HEBERLING, First Vice-President.
M. B. COCHRAN, Second Vice-President.
E. J. BABCOCK, Secretary.
P. E. SHAFER, Treasurer.

The following named comrades were selected as Executive Committee:

William Goodin, A; E. T. Hopkins, B; C. M. Turner, C; George M. Walker, D; E. T. Patterson, E; Cary R. Smith, F; E. S. Foster, G; A. U. McCormick, H; J. A. Donnell, I; John Fitzsimmons, K; A. G. Essen, L; A. H. Darwin, M.

Upon motion of Captain Reynolds, a vote of thanks was tendered the Executive Committee of this, our first reunion, for their work in making it a success.

Major Whisenand conducted the President-elect, D. A. Kerr, to the chair, who then addressed the association.

It was moved, and carried, that the proceedings of this reunion, and the regimental history, as presented by M. B. Cochran, be published.

On motion, Major John McDermott, Captains E. S. Foster, J. R. Perry, H. S. Heberling, and Major W. H. Whisenand, were appointed a committee on resolutions.

On motion, adjourned to meet at the parlors of the Kimball House at 8 o'clock, P. M.

E. S. FOSTER, *President.*

P. H. FRANCIS, *Secretary.*

The regiment was invited by the Veterans' Association to take dinner with them in camp, at the fair grounds, and, immediately after adjournment, they formed in columns of twos and marched to the grounds, escorted by Company B, I. N. G., and the Great Western band.

Tables had been provided, and an abundant supply of pork, beans, hard-tack, and coffee, with a plenty of sundries ; and they thoroughly enjoyed a regular camp-dinner.

After dinner the regiment united with the Veterans' Association in a grand parade through the streets of Davenport, returning to the fair grounds at 3 P. M., and listened to speeches from Colonel Benson, Hon. J. W. Green, and General John A. Logan.

THURSDAY EVENING.

The regiment met at the Kimball House.

The committee appointed at the morning session reported the following resolutions, which were unanimously adopted :

WHEREAS, The people of Davenport have, by their loyal devotion to the cause of the soldier, which is our common cause —the cause of liberty—re-endeared themselves to us by their open demonstration of joy in welcoming us to their midst in this, our first reunion, be it

Resolved, That we express to them, as we do to our beloved country, true soldierly devotion to the defense of right ; and we hereby desire and express to them our most hearty thanks and assurance of our grateful appreciation of all the kindness shown us on this occasion.

Resolved, That the fraternal feeling expressed by the cordial invitation of August Wentz Post to participate with them in the reunion of the Eastern Iowa Veteran Association, meets with most hearty response of fraternal relationship in our own hearts.

Resolved, That Company B, of the Second Regiment, Iowa National Guards, shall be held in honor by us for their deep fraternal greeting in giving us the free use of their commodious and pleasant hall, and their devoted attention at the reception at the opera house.

Resolved, That Professor Theodore Cramer and his male chorus have placed us under a willing contribution for their well-rendered and appropriate songs at the reception.

Resolved, That to all the railroads of Iowa (with the exception of the Illinois Central), we are under obligations for reduced rates of fare, and to the Chicago, Rock Island, & Pacific and the Chicago, Milwaukee, & St. Paul we tender our special thanks for free trains, to visit Rock Island arsenal and the Orphan's Home.

Resolved, That we return sincere thanks to Colonel D. W. Flagler, commanding Rock Island arsenal, and to the Trustees and Superintendent of the Orphan's Home, for their invitation to visit the arsenal and the home, and for other courtesies shown.

Resolved, That the Press of the state, in general, and *especially* the Press of Davenport, deserve more than common mention for proclaiming the news so freely and generously over the land, that the old soldiers of the First Iowa Cavalry were to meet in the goodly city of Davenport; and to them, in a very large measure, should be accorded the great success of this meeting.

Resolved, That comrades David A. Kerr, E. J. Babcock, E. L. Dean, M. B. Cochran, James Hill, and William Goodwin, all members of the Executive Committee, have shown their unselfish and undying devotion to their old comrades by the most arduous and continued labor for months, without hope of fee or reward, in bringing about this grand reunion, which has proved such a blessing to us all, in doubly-cementing our old fraternal ties.

Resolved, That we do most sincerely regret that we have not been permitted to meet, on this occasion, all our old comrades, who are living in various parts of this united country; but we cherish the fond hope that at our next reunion, three years from now, at some favored locality, we may all be permitted to meet, to greet, and to revive dear old memories.

> E. S. FOSTER,
> T. J. R. PERRY,
> JOHN McDELMOTT,
> H. HEBERLING,
> W. H. WHISENAND.

The report was received and adopted, and the committee discharged.

It was moved by Dr. Cochran that the Secretary be authorized to have blank applications for membership and notices of organization printed, and forwarded to all members of the regiment whose address could be obtained. Adopted.

On motion of Captain E. S. Foster, Messrs. Babcock, Cochran, and Hopkins were appointed a Committee on Publication, and empowered to have the full proceedings of this, our first reunion, with the regimental history, published as soon as practicable, and to forward one copy to each member of this association, and that the Secretary be authorized to draw a warrant on the Treasurer for payment of same.

A resolution was adopted requesting any person or member of the regiment having flags, guidons, or other articles of interest to the regiment' to donate the same to the association.

Letters were read from many former officers and members of the regiment, regretting their inability to be present at this, our first reunion, and promising attendance at the next one.

Among the letters, was one from R. B. Fulton, enclosing the following resolutions:

> "CAMP SHERIDAN,
> "HASTINGS, NEB., September 6th, 1883.

"We, the ex-members of the First Iowa Volunteer Cavalry, assembled, have hereby entered into a temporary organization, with Captain W. A. Coulter as Chairman, and R. B. Fulton as

Secretary, for the purpose of extending our congratulations and fraternal greetings to our old comrades-in-arms assembled at the reunion at Davenport, Iowa.

" *Resolved,* That we sincerely regret that circumstances prevent us from participating in the reunion ceremonies and festivities, and once more grasping the friendly hands of our old comrades.

" *Resolved,* That we but feebly express our heart-felt emotions through this medium, when we bid our dear old comrades *God speed* and a united and harmonious reunion.

" *Resolved,* That we entertain for our old comrades-in-arms that deep-seated and undying affection and fraternal feeling that time alone can efface; which grows stronger and stronger as the years roll around, each succeeding year intensifying those memories of hardships and blood-cemented friendship, engendered by trials which *tried* men's souls; investing their honored memories with a halo of patriotic glory — with a brilliancy that will never fade while ' reason sits enthroned, or memory holds its sway.'

" *Resolved,* That we most earnestly desire the unlimited success, not only of the reunion, but the personal prosperity of its several members, and express the hope that their deliberations, their camp-fires, their social intercourse, their greetings, and their partings may be characterized by earnestness, sobriety, and patriotic zeal, as behooves the defenders of our common country

" *Resolved,* That the proud distinction of having been a soldier for the preservation of the union, is the grandest heritage we can bequeath to posterity, and the consciousness of duty performed, and the discharge of important trusts committed to our care, as an integral part of the army of the south-west is a sufficient reward for the true soldier.

" *Resolved,* That we contemplate with sadness, the destitute condition of many of our old comrades, while the treasury of the United States — *their country!* — is literally overflowing with wealth, earned by their privations and blood; withholding from them the common comforts of life, while their wants could be relieved without any additional burden to the country.

" *Resolved,* That we hold in profound reverence the memories of the honored dead, and will cherish their remembrance and

6

protect their widows and orphans, as a sacred and holy duty
devolving upon us.

" 1. R. B. Fulton, Company B, Red Cloud, Nebraska.
" 2. George Rouse, " B, Kearney, Nebraska.
" 3. O. T. Johnson, " B, Belvidere, Thayer Co., Nebraska.
" 4. C. L. Kincaid, " E, Hastings, Nebraska.
" 5. W. Klingaman, " E, Ayer, Nebraska.
" 6. E. H. Bartlett, " E, Hastings, Nebraska.
" 7. Wm. Van Hoosen, " I, Beaver City, Nebraska.
" 8. W. Hawk, " I, Beaver City, Nebraska.
" 9. Jo. Springer, " I, Carrolton, Thayer Co., Nebraska.
" 10. J. D. Dodge, " I, Prairie View, Kansas.
" 11. D. H. Ferman, " H, Wilbur, Nebraska
" 12. J. H. Ferman, " H, Red Cloud, Nebraska.
" 13. J. C. Allen, " H, Superior, Nebraska.
" 14. R. Wescott, " H, Juniata, Nebraska.
" 15. John Lyon, " A, Davenport, Nebraska.
" 16. M. D. Copp. " A, Wahoo, Saunders Co., Nebraska.
" 17. L. S. Drinkwater, " G, Prairie Star, Kansas.
" 18. W. Kortz, " F, Crete, Nebraska.
" 19. C. M. Slade, " L, Lincoln, Nebraska.
" 20. J. C. Delbridge, " D, Cambridge, Furnas Co., Nebraska.
" 21. W. A. Coulter, Mt. Pleasant, Iowa.

" W. A. COULTER, *Chairman.*
" R. B. FULTON, *Secretary.*"

FRIDAY.

Friday morning, on the invitation of Colonel D. W. Flagler, the regiment visited Rock Island arsenal, and were shown the works and buildings in process of construction there. H. H. Hills, Esq., agent of the Chicago, Rock Island, & Pacific Railway, kindly tendered an engine and cars to take the members to the island.

In the afternoon the "boys" witnessed the sham-battle of the Veterans' Association, which came as near the genuine article as it is hoped they will ever be held, and which showed conclusively that those who participated in it "had been there," and knew "how to do it."

The best of feeling prevailed throughout the entire reunion, and all felt amply repaid for the sacrifice they had made in attending.

On motion adjourned, to meet in three years, on call of the Executive Committee.

D. A. KERR, *President.*

E. J. BABCOCK, *Secretary.*

NOTE.—I wish to make due acknowledgement to Col. D. Anderson Capts. J. R. Ellis, S. S. Burdett, and E. S. Foster, Lieut. J. M. Simeral, Adjt. D. A. Kerr, and E. T. Hopkins, for valuable information regarding the organization of their respective companies, and to the very full history of the regiment by Col. A. G. McQueen, contained in the Adjutant-General's report.

For full correspondence relating to orders Nos. 2 and 15, see report of Adjutant-General of Iowa, page 514, Vol. 2, 1867.

M. B. COCHRAN.

DAVENPORT, Sept. 25th, 1883.

NOTE.—It is earnestly desired that all who were ever members of the First Iowa Cavalry, and who were honorably discharged from service, shall become members of the association; and any member of the regiment whose name and address is not recorded in this publication will please inform the Secretary, or any member of the Executive Committee.

Members of the First Iowa Cavalry Association.

FIELD AND STAFF.

Albers, C. H..St. Louis, Mo.
Cochran, M. B...Davenport, Iowa.
Chase, Levi..San Diego, Cal.
Donnell, J. A..Sigourney, Iowa.
Kerr, David A...Keokuk, Iowa.
King, Jas. L...Springfield, Ill.
Lothrop, Chas. H......................................Lyons, Iowa.
Ladd, J. A...Traer, Iowa.
McDermott, John..Dubuque, Iowa.
Marshall, J. L...Morning Sun, Iowa.
Morrill, Henry L.......................................Saratoga Springs, Iowa.
Rand, J. S...Council Bluffs, Iowa.
Whisenand, W. S..Ottawa, Iowa.

COMPANY A.

Babcock, E. J..Davenport, Iowa.
Carter, Chas. A..Bentonsport, Iowa.
Carter, Wm. H..Bentonsport, Iowa.
Conn, O. L...Keokuk, Iowa.
Cheesman, Michael......................................Montrose, Iowa.
Dwigans, Joseph..Stuart, Iowa.
Ferrell, Isaac...Morning Sun, Iowa.
Ford, Jonathan...Wilton, Iowa.
Goodin, Wm...Farmington, Iowa.
Gray, W. S...Keokuk, Iowa.
Gabriel, Hiram...Keokuk, Iowa.
Hill, James..Keokuk, Iowa.
Henkle, John...Afton, Iowa.
Jones, Frank H...Keokuk, Iowa.
Johnston, Jas. E.......................................Musselshell, M. T.
Lyon, John C...Davenport, Neb.
McKey, Geo. W..Howard, Kansas.
McCandlass, Jos. C.....................................Sonora, Ill.

Moss, C. E..Kansas, Mo.
Miller, George R...Albia, Iowa.
Nelson, N. P...Keokuk, Iowa.
Osborn, A. H...New Liberty, Iowa.
Oblenness, L. L..Keokuk, Iowa.
Reynolds, R. M..Washington, D. C.
Reynolds, Thomas...Confidence, Iowa.
Russell, J. L...Prairie City, Iowa.
Reibold, Daniel...Terre Haute, Ind.
Reed, Elmore..Montrose, Iowa.
Rosecrans, Lewis...Braddyville, Iowa.
Rosecrans, L. W...Williamstown, Mo.
Rhodes, Leonard W...North Granville, N. Y.
Sala, Orland P..Bloomington, Wis.
Sweet, E. L..Greely, Iowa.
Sala, A. F..Keokuk, Iowa.
Shook, Jacob M..Scottsville, Kansas.
Smith John W..Washta, Iowa.
Scheyli, Wm..Gabriel Mills, Tex.
Thomas, Z. E...Washington, D. C.
Torrence, F. G..Birmingham, Iowa.
Thatcher, Aaron H..Mt. Sterling, Iowa.
Thorndike, Wm. F..Salem, Mass.
Walker, Add...Washington, D. C.
Wyatt, Wm. H..Keokuk, Iowa.
Wright, John, No. 1...Keokuk, Iowa.
Wilson, A. J...Austin, Neb.
Wilson, J. S..Golden, Col.

COMPANY B.

Adams, Nicholas...Elkader, Iowa.
Bullock, D. S..Lost Nation, Iowa.
Burdett, S. S..Washington, D. C.
Chattield, M. M..Rock Rapids, Iowa.
Elliott, R. M..Kansas City, Mo.
Francis, Phil. H..Cedar Rapids, Iowa.
Forbes, Daniel M..De Witt, Iowa.
Foster, J. T..Lyons, Iowa.
Gulie, Isaac...State Center, Iowa.
Hopkins, E. T..Davenport, Iowa.
Heberling, H. S..Marion, Iowa.
McMillan, D. S...Oxford Junction, Iowa.
Rhodes, Isaac...DeWitt, Iowa.
Smith, E. J...Sedalia, Mo.
Smith, E. H..Dubuque, Iowa.
Tate, W. G...Chicago, Ills.

Williams, D. W..Kansas City, Mo.
West, W. H. H..DeWitt, Iowa.
Woodward, B. S..Lyons, Iowa.

COMPANY C.

Boltz, Joseph..Morning Sun, Iowa.
Copp, C. M..Wahoo, Neb.
Klein, Max..Pittsburgh, Penn.
Mellinger, John..Morning Sun, Iowa.
Patterson, G. W..Mediapolis, Iowa.
Perry, T. J. R..Riverton, Iowa.
Payne, Horace..Geneva, Ohio.
Steele, W. S..Butler, Mo.
Seyb, Michael..Kahoka, Mo.
Swan, R. M..Burlington, Iowa.
Stutsman, A. H..Burlington, Iowa.
Turner, C. M..Burlington, Iowa.
Vanfleet, James..Flaglers, Iowa.

COMPANY D.

Creswell, J. M..Grandview, Iowa.
Cory, Johnathan..Augusta, Iowa.
Cory, John..Augusta, Iowa.
Delbridge, J. C..Arapahoe, Neb.
Grant, W. K..Danville, Iowa.
Graham, John W..Winterset, Iowa.
Hornby, W. L..Denmark, Iowa.
James, Elias..Marshalltown, Iowa.
McClelland, J. L..Winterset, Iowa.
Pitger, J. W..Ravenswood, Fla.
Palmer, S. B..Marshalltown, Iowa.
Stewart, W. H..Danville, Iowa.
Strodley, G. P..Swan, Iowa.
Walker, Geo. M..Des Moines, Iowa.

COMPANY E.

Campbell, J. A..Severance, Kansas.
Howe, S. H..Columbus City Iowa.
Hall, I. W..Columbus, Kansas.
Limbocker, Orlando C..Morning Sun, Iowa.
Patterson, T. E..Anamosa, Iowa.

COMPANY F.

Allen, J. S..Argonia, Kansas.
Bunker, Jesse..Gilmore, Mich.

Boyd, Daniel..... ....South Amana, Iowa.
Corlett, John ....Anita, Iowa.
Clark, W. H..Volga City.
Foster, E. N...Wellman, Iowa.
Hart, George..Denmark, Iowa.
Hart, T. H...Denmark, Iowa.
Hart, R. S............................... ....Denmark, Iowa.
Hise, J. G.................................... .. ..Washington, Iowa.
Hoxie, R. S................................... ....Washington, D. C.
Hurlburt, M. W...Sylvan Grove, Kans.
Huskins, J. C.... ....Brighton, Iowa.
McCormick, J. W.................. ....Wellman, Iowa.
Morgan, D. E ....Tower Hill, Ill.
Matthews, J. L......... ....Wellman, Iowa.
Myers, Chas...Wellman, Iowa.
Morrow, John A....................... ....Waterville, Kans.
Powers, Albert ....Wellman, Iowa.
Roso, S. W.. ....Fairbank, Iowa.
Shaver, P. E..Amish, Iowa.
Smith, Carey R.. ...Iowa City, Iowa.
Sumner, J. R...Oakland, Cal.
Smelseer, C...................... ....Richmond, Iowa.
Woodruff, Chalmer P..Columbus City, Ia.

COMPANY G.

Armitage, J. P................................. ....Glidden, Iowa.
Alline, A. A.. ....Le Mars, Iowa.
Buswell, Geo. R...Lovelock, Neb.
Brown, Ed. J...Quincy, Ill.
Foster, E. S..Audubon, Iowa.
Fish, Wm. B..Anamosa, Iowa.
Gregory, Henry...Jackson, Iowa.
Krapfel, J. W...Waterloo, Iowa.
Lounsberry, Joel...Union, Iowa.
Morgan, A...Greely, Iowa.
Stone, Jas. L...Delhi, Iowa.
Scott, D. W..Maquoketa, Iowa.
Skinner, Benj. F...Manchester, Iowa.
Schoonover, L...Anamosa, Iowa.
Trenchard, S. W.. ....Manchester, Iowa.
Thompson, John S. B.......................................Grundy Center, Iowa.
Welles, E. L..Wallace, Kansas.

COMPANY H.

Cowans, Wm. H.................. ....Flaglers, Iowa.
Carrol, Nathan A...Melrose, Iowa.
Hodge, D...Ottumwa, Iowa.

COMPANY I.

Crocker, B. F..Martinsburg, Iowa.
Daly, Frank...Pontoosic, Ill.
Dinsmore, D. C...Kirkville, Iowa.
Donnell, O. H..Hedrick, Iowa.
Donnell, S. H..Martinsburg, Iowa.
Donnell, R. L..Sigourney, Iowa.
Hawk, Ezra..Martinsburg, Iowa.
Johnson, A. J...Martinsburg, Iowa.
McAuley, William.......................................Pontoosic, Ill.
Myers, T. J...Burlington, Iowa.
Phelps, A. R..Competine, Iowa.
Sylvester, Geo. W.......................................Competine, Iowa.
Thompson, E. C...Agency City, Iowa.
Walker, S. C..Batavia, Iowa.

COMPANY K.

Atwood, C. P..Anamosa, Iowa.
Barnes, Thos. H..Wankon, Iowa.
Casey, M...Durham, Iowa.
Fitzsimmons, John......................................Monticello, Iowa.
Herriman, W. B...Wadena, Iowa.
Jones, Allen...Buffalo, Iowa.
Keeler, Chas...Chicago, Ill.
Phelan, James..Anamosa, Iowa.
Russell, J. M..Mill Bunn, Penn.
Swingle, N. M..Muscatine, Iowa.

COMPANY L.

Bunn, Caleb..Halestine, Iowa.
Chase, C. A..Rochester, N. Y.
Essen, C. G..Dubuque, Iowa.
Foote, W. M..Preston, Minn.
Guthrie, W. L..Golden, Iowa.
Jordan, M. V...Lettsville, Iowa.
Jones, E. R..Wankon, Iowa.
Lafrance, L..Dubuque, Iowa.
Lewis, Geo...Grenola, Kansas.
Miller, Chas. E..Severance, Kans.
Mead, H. H...Dubuque, Iowa.
Miller, Andrew...Manchester, Iowa.
Maurice, N...Monticello, Iowa.
Manwaring, L. B..Wheatland, Iowa.
Stoneman, Lewis..Denison, Texas.
Thomas, A. B...Ames, Iowa.
Wise, John...Bellevue, Iowa.

7

COMPANY M.

Boyd, Joseph..Davenport, Iowa.
Darwin, A. H..Lyons, Iowa.
Dierks, Hans..Lyons, Iowa.
Deane, L. E...Lyons, Iowa.
Grandy, John...Nora Springs, Iowa.
Gaston, A. D...Ames, Iowa.
Hathaway, W. W..Davenport, Iowa.
Hills, W. W..Madison, Dakota.
Rigby, W. H..Mechanicsville, Iowa.
Stuhr, John..Rock Island, Ills.
Wirth, Joseph..Angus, Iowa
Wilkes, F. R...McCook, Neb.
Nettles, Geo. T..Perry, Iowa.

NAMES AND ADDRESS

The Surviving Members of the First Iowa Cavalry,

AS FAR AS KNOWN.

FIELD AND STAFF OFFICERS.

Anderson, Daniel, Colonel........................Albia, Iowa.
Thompson, Wm., Colonel........................Bismark, Dak. T.
Moss, Chas. F., Lieutenant-Colonel........................Emporia, Kans.
Bryan, P. Gad, Lieutenant-Colonel........................Des Moines, Iowa.
McQueen, A. G., Lieutenant-Colonel........................Flora, Ills.
Jenks, J. D., Major........................Butte City, M. T.
Chase, Levi, Major........................Los Angeles, Cal.
*Whisenand, W. S., Major........................Ottawa, Kans.
*McDermott, John, Major........................Dubuque, Iowa.
Bereman, Major........................Mt. Pleasant, Iowa.
*Cochran, M. B., Surgeon........................Davenport, Iowa.
*Lathrop, C. H., Surgeon........................Lyons, Iowa.
Allen, D. B., Assistant Surgeon........................West Liberty, Ohio.
Morgan, Asa, Assistant Surgeon........................Cedar Bayou, Tex.
Hervey, J. L., Assistant Surgeon........................Dubuque, Iowa.
*Ladd, J. A., Assistant Surgeon........................Traer, Iowa.
Stone, J. C., Adjutant........................Burlington, Iowa.
*Kerr, David A., Adjutant........................Keokuk, Iowa.
Donnell, J. A., Adjutant........................Sigourney, Iowa.
Morrell, H. L., Adjutant........................Hoosic Tunnell, Mass.
Bryan, J. M., Adjutant........................Audubon, Iowa.
McClure, W. P., Quarter-Master........................Topeka, Kansas.
*Albers, C. Henri, Quarter-Master........................St. Louis, Mo.
Fluke, W. W., Quarter-Master........................Lawrence, Kansas.
Dashiel, H. L., Commissary-Sergeant........................Albia, Kansas.
Newel, Robt., Commissary-Sergeant........................Chetopa, Kansas.
*Rand, J. S., Chaplain........................Council Bluffs, Iowa.
Elder, Thos. H., Hospital Steward........................Albia, Iowa.
Delfelder, Geo., Hospital Steward........................Tipton, Mo.
Edwards, Baron, Hospital Steward........................Chetopa, Kans.
*King, Jas. L., B. S. M........................Springfield, Ill.

---

*Present at the reunion.

Easley, Dan, Quarter-Master's-Sergeant..............Confidence, Iowa.
Cheesman, M., B. V. S..............................Montrose, Iowa.
Cunningham, A. G., Bugler.......................Little Rock, Arks.
Hall, W. B., Bugler...........................Columbus City, Iowa.
Marshall, J. L., Band...........................Morning Sun, Iowa.

FIRST IOWA CAVALRY ROSTER.

COMPANY A.

*Reynolds, R. M., Captain.......................Washington, D. C.
Oblenness, T. J., Captain......................Alexandria, Mo.
Boyce, A. P., Lieutenant.......................Sterling, Kansas.
*Russell, J. L., Lieutenant....................Prairie City, Iowa.
Turner, Jas. P., Lieutenant....................Keokuk, Iowa.
Andrews, Wm. C................................Montrose, Iowa.
*Babcock, E. J.................................Davenport, Iowa.
Blair, Benjamin...............................Sterling, Kansas.
Blair, Wm. W..................................Menomonee, Wis.
Bridges, Brainard, Corporal....................Shelby, Ohio.
Carter, Alex..................................Bentonsport, Iowa.
*Carter, Wm...................................Bentonsport, Iowa.
Clapp, M. D...................................Wahoo, Neb.
*Copp, M. D...................................Wahoo, Neb.
Davis, Frank..................................Andover, Mo.
*Dwigans, Joseph..............................Stuart, Iowa.
*Ford, Jonathan...............................Wilton, Iowa.
Fort, John B..................................Bodie, Cal.
*Ferrill, Isaac...............................Morning Sun, Iowa.
*Gray, Walter S., Sergeant.....................Keokuk, Iowa.
*Goodin, Wm., Corporal.........................Farmington, Iowa.
Gabriel, Hiram................................Keokuk, Iowa.
Hill, James...................................Keokuk, Iowa.
Huiskamp, H. J................................Ft. Madison, Iowa.
Horton, Wm....................................Montrose, Iowa.
Green, Geo. W.................................Conway, Iowa.
*Jones, Frank H...............................Keokuk, Iowa.
Johnston, Jas. E..............................Mussellshell, M. T.
Kennedy, Alex.................................Gregory's Landing, Mo.
Lyons, Chas. H................................Dexter, Iowa.
Lyon, John C..................................Davenport, Neb.
Merrill, H. S.................................Saratoga Springs, N. Y.
*Moss, Chas. E., Jr...........................Kansas City, Mo.
McCandless, Jos. C., Corporal..................Sonora, Ills.
McKilben, Chas................................Keokuk, Iowa.
Miller, Geo. R................................Belinda, Iowa.
*McKey, Geo. W................................Howard, Kansas.

Nelson, Peter...Keokuk, Iowa.
Newell, Samuel H................................ ....Eddyville, Iowa.
Oiler, Eli R.................... ....Keokuk, Iowa.
Oblenness, L. L., Corporal............................Keokuk, Iowa.
Oblenness, Andrew......................................Topeka, Kansas.
*Osborn, Alex............................... ......New Liberty, Iowa.
*Reibold, Daniel......... ....Terre Haute, Ind.
*Reed, Elmore..... ....Montrose, Iowa.
Russell, John.......... ....Montrose, Iowa.
Rosecranz, L. W... .... Wayland, Mo.
Rhodes, L. W ....North Grinville N. Y.
*Reynolds, Thomas, Corporal............................Confidence, Iowa.
Renflin, George..Chicago, Ills.
*Sala, Anglos F..Keokuk, Iowa.
Seabolt, Elihu..St. Joseph, Mo.
Seabolt, Edward..St. Josesh, Mo.
*Sala, Orlando P..Bloomington, Wis.
Short, Lewis E..Shell City, Mo.
Scott, James..Great Bend, Kansas.
Scheyli, Wm..South Gabriel, Tex.
*Sweet, E. L..Greeley, Iowa.
Smith, John, Bugler....................................Washta, Iowa.
*Shook, Jacob M...Scottsville, Kansas.
*Torrence, F. G..Birmingham, Iowa.
*Thomas, Z. E..Washington, D. C.
*Thatcher, Aaron A., Farrier............................Mt. Sterling, Iowa.
Turner, David C..Keokuk, Iowa.
Tuttle, Prentice, K......................................Hamilton, Ills.
Thorndike, Wm. F......................................Salem, Mass.
Vanaerman, A., Corp....................................Hamilton, Ills.
Vansant, J. S..Washington, D. C.
*Walker, Adison..Washington, D. C.
Wright, John, (2) Corp.................................Springfield, Mo.
*Wright, John (1) Corp.................................Keokuk, Iowa.
Welchymer, George....................................Montrose, Iowa.
Wilson, Walker..Montrose, Iowa.
Wilson, H. T..Le Claire, Iowa.
*Wyatt, Wm. H..Keokuk, Iowa.
Walker, F. J..Montrose, Iowa.
Wilson, A. J..Austin, Texas.
Wright, A. J..Diana, Kansas.
*Wilson, Harrison......................................Montrose, Iowa.
Wilson, Ishmall T................... ....Golden, Col.
Wisby, L. B............................. ....Omaha, Neb.
Wingrove, B. F..Westline, Kansas.

8

COMPANY B.

Burdett, S. S., Captain	Washington, D. C.
Leffingwell, Wm. E., Captain	Chicago, Ills.
*Foster, J. T. Captain	Lyons, Iowa.
Shiffer, Henry P., Lieutenant	Little Rock, Ark.
*Heberling, Hiram S., Lieutenant	Cedar Rapids, Iowa.
*Defriest, Wm. H. Lieutenant	Lyons, Iowa.
*Adams, Nicholas	Elkader, Iowa.
Buell, Strong, Sergeant	Arkansas City, Ark.
*Bullock, D. S.	Lost Nation, Iowa.
Bias, Francis	Harrisburg, Mo.
Bodell, R. M.	Waterloo, Iowa.
Coe, John A.	Milledgeville, Ill.
Crawford, T. M.	Monona, Iowa.
Carney, Geo. R.	Monroe, Iowa.
Crandall, Henry C.	Strawberry Point, Ia.
Chatfield, M. M.	Rock Rapids, Iowa.
Cunningham, M.	Volga City, Iowa.
Darling, Lemuel	St. Louis, Mo.
*Downing, John	Andrew, Iowa.
Durling, Wm.	St. Louis, Mo.
Evans, L. H.	Denver, Col.
Emery, Silas H.	Thompson, Iowa.
Ely, T.	Elkader, Iowa.
*Elliott, R. M.	Kansas City, Mo.
Fulton, R. B., Sergeant	Red Cloud, Neb.
*Forbes, Daniel W.	DeWitt, Iowa.
*Francis, P. H.	Cedar Rapids, Iowa.
*Gates, John M., Sergeant	Grand Mound, Iowa.
Gardner, W. W., Corporal	Lost Nation, Iowa.
*Gulic, Isaac, Corporal	State Center, Iowa.
*Hopkins, E. T., Bugler	Davenport, Iowa.
*Hurlburt, Augustus	Lyons, Iowa.
Johnson, Otis T.	Belvidere, Neb.
Keller, John	Richmond Neb.
Lister, James, Corporal	Morrison, Ills.
Leonard, H. J.	Beloit, Wis.
*McMillan, D. S.	Oxford Junction, Iowa.
McKeen, John	Green Springs, Ohio.
Moore, Richard	Rock Creek, Kansas.
Miller, John A., Corporal	Ft. Bayard, N. M.
Pierson, Luke	Rising, Neb.
*Rhodes, Isaac	DeWitt, Iowa.
Rull, Freeman	Lyons, Iowa.
Robinson, Frank H.	Morrison Ills.
Rouse, John	Kearney, Neb.
Smith, E. H.	Dubuque, Iowa.

Stanley, Charles..St. Louis, Mo.
Stanley, E. G...Dubuque, Iowa.
Stockwell, H. B..Clinton, Iowa.
*Smith, E. J., Corporal..Sedalia, Mo.
Soper, W. L., Corporal...Hot Springs, Ark.
Saxton, James..DeWitt, Iowa.
*Tyler, George E., Blacksmith...............................Grand Mound, Iowa.
*Tate, William G...Chicago, Ills.
Truman, S..Strawberry Point, Ia.
Tietjens, J. H..Indian Grove, Mo.
*West, W. H. H..DeWitt, Iowa.
*Williams, Warren...Chetopa, Kansas.
Walker, John O..Greenville, Ills.
*Woodward, B. S., Sergeant..................................Lyons, Iowa.

COMPANY C.

*Perry, T. J. R., Captain......................................Hamburg, Iowa.
*Turner, Clinton M., Lieutenant.............................Burlington, Iowa.
Clark, Wm. A., Lieutenant...................................Burlington, Iowa.
Vanbeek, George, Lieutenant................................New London, Iowa.
Ronaldson, M., Lieutenant...................................Pierre, Dakota.
Atherton, S..Denver, Col.
Barr, George..Salt Lake City, Utah.
Brandt, John..Augusta, Iowa.
Boman, A. W...Leon, Iowa.
Boyer, Michael...Wapello, Iowa.
*Boltz, Joseph..Morning Sun, Iowa.
Brice, Albert C...Lenox, Iowa.
Craig, Walter..Kansas, City, Mo.
*Copp, C. M..Wahoo, Neb.
Chapman, S. P...Wapello, Iowa.
Castle, B. S., Sergeant.,......................................Johnstown, Ohio.
Carter, J. D...Chariton, Iowa.
Carter, Jackson, Sergeant....................................St. Louis, Mo.
*Dellfelder, George...Tipton, Mo.
Horner, Lloyd..Little Rock, Ark.
Hawkins, Geo. C...Creston, Iowa.
Hendricks, Paul, Corporal...................................Bustes, Mo.
Hutchinson, Thomas..Burlington, Iowa.
Hook, George...Memphis, Tenn.
Hammond J..Augusta, Kansas.
Ingersoll, James..Huron, Iowa.
Johnston, L. B..Burlington, Iowa.
Jefferson, H...West Point, Iowa.
Kitchen, Jerry..Burlington, Iowa.
Keaver, W. O. P...Orsburg, Mo.
Morris, Martin C...Arcolia, Mo.

Moore, Martin, Corporal..Topeka, Kansas.
*Mellinger, John...Morning Sun, Iowa.
Majors, E. W..Girard, Kansas.
*Payne, Horace...Mechanicsville, Ohio.
Parkinson, S. D...Trenton, Mo.
*Patterson, George W.....................................Mediapolis, Iowa.
Ritchey, Joe...Des Moines, Iowa..
Smith, Wm. B...Burlington, Iowa.
*Swan, Mark..Burlington, Iowa.
Shelton, Wm. P...Desoto, Missouri.
*Stutsman, A. H..Burlington, Iowa.
*Seyb, Michael...Kahoka, Missouri.
Storey, Nick...Burlington, Iowa.
Slocum, Wm. H...Quincy, Ill.
*Steele, Wm. S..Butler, Mo.
Stoddard, Allen..West Point, Iowa.
Shaak, Jacob...Scottsville, Kansas.
Turner, C. M., Corporal..................................Burlington, Iowa.
*Vanfleet, James..Flaglers, Iowa.
Welsch, Samuel B...Middletown, Iowa.
Wilson, Samuel F...Mediapolis, Iowa.
Wilson, T. D..Lacona, Iowa.

COMPANY D.

*Walker, George M., Captain..............................Des Moines, Iowa.
Shriver, Wm. R., Lieutenant..............................Winterset, Iowa.
Hammon, John C., Lieutenant..............................Spring Hill, Iowa.
Butler, J. G., Lieutenant................................Boulder, Col.
Barlow, John...Chariton, Iowa.
Bird, Butler..Bermington, Iowa.
Brown, A. Z...Fredonia, Kansas.
Carpenter, Willet..Indianola, Iowa.
Carter, Milton, sadler...................................Afton, Iowa.
Conrad, Samuel M...Milo, Iowa.
Crosthwait, Perry, Sergeant..............................Des Moines, Iowa.
Carter, W. C..Atlantic, Iowa.
Delbridge, J. C...Cambridge, Neb.
Franches, Jack..Ohio, Iowa.
Grant, W. K...Danville, Iowa.
Griffith, B. F..Warrensburg, Mo.
Hornby, Wm. L...Denmark, Iowa.
Hill, Peter...Seuyler, Neb.
Hammon, Levi..Indianola, Iowa.
Harsh, Jacob..New Virginia, Iowa.
Hammond, Henry D..Topeka, Kansas.
Imes, W..Patterson, Iowa.
Judkins, Milton..Indianola, Iowa.

Judkins, Van B...Indianola, Iowa.
Judkins, J...Indianola, Iowa.
Kelley, D. C..Omaha, Neb.
Kelly, R. W..Fayette, Iowa.
Lewis, Charles V...Derby, Iowa.
Lowry, James...Shenandoah, Iowa.
Ledington, G. W..McPherson, Kansas.
May, Tobias...Coffeyville, Kansas.
*McClelland, J. L...Peru, Iowa.
Roberts, David...Plumb Creek, Neb.
Reed, S..Winterset, Iowa.
Shannon, Samuel E., Corporal........................Atlantic, Iowa.
Sydebotham, Jabez......................................Derby, Iowa.
Stewart, W. H...Danville, Iowa.
Slough, Jesse...North Jackson, Ohio.
Smith, Jackson C...Cora, Kansas.
Sampson, Carlos, Corporal.............................Patterson, Iowa.
Shannon, Enoch, Corporal..............................Atlantic, Iowa.
Shoemaker, D. C..Battle Creek, Kansas.
Turk, William, Corporal.................................Bermington, Iowa.
Trumble, Enoch...Indianola, Iowa.
Wilson, William...Osceola, Iowa.
*Wilson, C. S..Des Moines, Iowa.
Williams, John H..Cedar Rapids, Iowa.

COMPANY E.

Coulter, William A., Captain............................Mt. Pleasant, Iowa.
Ives, George E., Lieutenant.............................Mt. Pleasant, Iowa.
Kauffman, C. C., Lieutenant............................Mobile, Alabama.
Baxter, Robert, Lieutenant..............................Knoxville, Iowa.
Butlington, J. J..Salem, Iowa.
Bean, Thomas M..Eagle Rock, Idaho.
Brown, Alexander...Cherokee, Iowa.
Bigler, Theodore..Mt. Pleasant, Iowa.
Bereman, T. H...La Hayb, Iowa.
Bumgardner, D. C., Wagoner...........................Pueblo, Colorado.
Bird, C. M., Corporal.....................................Afton, Iowa.
Blazer, J. H., Sergeant...................................Ft. Station, N. M.
Bartlett, E. H..Hastings, Neb.
Coates, G. F..Phœnix, Arizona T.
Cromwell, Arthur...New London, Iowa.
Cantebury, C..New London, Iowa.
*Colville, B. P...Monmouth, Ills.
Campbell, James A.......................................Severance, Kansas.
Cratty, William...Burlington, Iowa.
Craig, W. P..Trenton, Mo.
Gray, William...Mt. Pleasant, Iowa.
9

Hephrey, Daniel..Anthony, Kansas.
*Howe, Samuel..Columbus City, Iowa.
Helphrey, F. P..Mt. Pleasant, Iowa.
Howard, C. M..New London, Iowa.
Hess, H. H..Salem, Iowa.
Haggett, Isaac H..Salem, Iowa.
Ives, Nathaniel, Bugler..Cedar Rapids, Iowa.
Jobes, Charles..Seward, Neb.
Klingman, W..Ayer, Neb.
Kempton, G. W..Loveland, Col.
Kincaid, Orlando D..Abilene, Texas.
Kitchen, Jeremiah..Burlington, Iowa.
Kelley, James L..Springfield, Ills.
Kincaid, C. L..Hastings, Neb.
*Limbocker, O. C..Morning Sun, Iowa.
Lynch, Clarke..Mt. Pleasant, Iowa.
Lyman, Gad..New London, Iowa.
McCormick, John..Wichita, Kansas.
Mathews, J. R..Salem, Iowa.
North, John T., Sergeant..Winfield, Iowa.
Pricket, Elias..New London, Iowa.
*Patterson, T. E..Anamosa, Iowa.
Pickard, Edward..Salem, Iowa.
Potter, J..Gunnison, Colorado.
Pickard, Hiram..Salem, Iowa.
Ramsey, Geo. W..New London, Iowa.
Roberts, Berryman..Keokuk, Iowa.
Stapleton, E. M..Kinsley, Kansas.
Snyder, C. M..Mt. Pleasant, Iowa.
Shampnoi, Thomas..Salem, Iowa.
Thompson, Samuel..Scottsville, Kansas.
*VanOrsdol, George W., Corporal..Silver Lake, Iowa.
Williams, O. M..Columbus, Kansas.
Worley, George W..Hopkins, Mo.
Wiggans, L. D..Wayland, Iowa.
Welweth, I. L..Salem, Iowa.
Weller, Charles, Corporal..New London, Iowa.
Walker, R..Utica, Iowa.

COMPANY F.

*Shaver, Philip E., Captain..Iowa City, Iowa.
*Elliott, J. R., Captain..Grand Junction, Col.
Dow, Charles W. W., Captain..Rushmore, Minn.
*Huskins, James C., Lieutenant..Brighton, Iowa.
Allen, A. B..Hazleton, Iowa.
Austin, L. W..Bazien, Kansas.
Bolton, John..Iowa City, Iowa.

Browner, N. H., Corporal..................................Cedar Bluffs, Kansas.
*Bunker, Jesse...Gilmore, Mich.
Bolding, W..Dorchester, Neb.
*Corlett, John..Iowa City, Iowa.
*Clark, W. H ....Volga City, Iowa.
Craig, L. R...Dennison City, Texas.
Doran, James B..Bedford, Iowa.
*Foster, E. N ....Wellman Iowa.
Fuller, Victor..Brush Creek, Iowa.
Hoxsie, R. L., Sergeant....................................Washington, D. C.
*Hart, Thomas H ....Denmark, Iowa.
*Hart, Ray S..Denmark, Iowa.
*Hart, George...Denmark, Iowa.
Hunter, J. C..Newton, Iowa.
Hamlin, Henry C. ....Colfax, N. M.
*Hise, Joseph G...Washington, Iowa.
Hiatt, Lewis..Columbus City, Iowa.
Helmick, William...Cairo, Iowa.
Hana, David ....Peoria, Ills.
Hayes, M..Hazelton, Iowa.
Hamilton, William F., Sergeant............................Palmer, Colorado.
Klein, Max..Pittsburgh, Penn.
Kortz, William R...Crete, Neb.
McCord, James H., Sergeant.................................Des Moines, Iowa.
McCord, D. M ....Newton, Iowa.
*Mayer, Charles...Wellman, Iowa.
*McCormick, J. W..Wellman, Iowa.
*Mathews, I. L..Wellman, Iowa.
McClure, William, Corporal...................................Richmond, Iowa.
McCoy, Charles A...St. Joseph, Mo.
*Morgan, D. E., Quarter-Master's Sergeant.................Tower Hill, Ills.
McClure, George..Alexandria, Nebraska.
Morrow, J. A..Waterville Kansas.
O'Conner, B...Elkader, Iowa.
*Powers, Albert...Wellman, Iowa.
Perry, H. B...Dell Norte, Colo.
Park Russell..Denmark, Iowa.
Platt, J..Oelwein, Iowa.
Ross, S. W..Fairbanks, Iowa.
*Roberts, J. B..Fairbanks, Iowa.
Sayles, W. O..Mill, Iowa.
Smith, Carey R., Corporal.....................................Iowa City, Iowa.
Straten, E. T...Iowa City, Iowa.
*Smelseer, E. T...Iowa City, Iowa.
*Sumner, J. R...Denver, Colo.
Stebbins, M...Waverly, Iowa.
Wyley, J. L...Greenville, Ohio.

*Woodruff, Chalmer P..........................Columbus City, Iowa.
Wildman, Ira H...............................Central City, Neb.
Wilson, I. P..................................Newton, Iowa.
Wilson, J. E., Corporal.......................Chamberlain, D. T.
*Young, R. J..................................Oelwein, Iowa.

COMPANY G.

Hosford, A. W., Captain.......................Rockdale, Iowa.
*Foster, E. S., Lieutenant.....................Audubon, Iowa.
Klingeberg, E. A., Lieutenant..................Milwaukee, Wis.
*Armitage, John...............................Glidden, Iowa.
Allen, George.................................Castalia, Iowa.
Alline, A. A., Sergeant........................Le Mars, Iowa.
*Brown, Edward, J.............................Quincy, Ills.
Byreley, Purdy M., Farrier.....................Farley, Iowa.
Buswell, George R., Corporal...................Lovelock, Nev.
. Bivins, Jeremiah.............................Orient, Iowa.
*Barto, C. M..................................Center Junction, Iowa.
Bradfield, H. A...............................Hubbard, Iowa.
Burk, Stephen.................................Eldora, Iowa.
Brownson, S. H................................Raymond, Iowa.
Babcock, W. W., Sergeant......................Eldora, Iowa.
Clinkenbeard, E. L............................Eldora, Iowa.
Druckathe, L. S...............................Prairie Star, Neb.
Dory, F. A....................................Idaho Springs, Colo.
Detrich, George...............................Brush Creek, Iowa.
Erwin, Joseph C., Bugler.......................Minneapolis, Minn.
Eggleston, C. B...............................Louisville, Colo.
Eggleston, W. K...............................Bonanza City, Colo.
*Fish, William B..............................Anamosa, Iowa.
Fowkes, Allen.................................Monticello, Iowa.
Furman, John M................................Eldora, Iowa.
Farmington, Stanton...........................Dubuque, Iowa.
Foulker, Allen................................Monticello, Iowa.
Gaut, Matthew.................................Wooster, Ohio.
Gorham, James.................................Douglass, Iowa.
*Gregory, Henry...............................Jackson, Mich.
Hanna, John Q.................................Goldfield, Iowa.
Hoover, Harris, Sergeant......................Clearfield, Pa.
Hull, Samuel R., Sergeant.....................Waterloo, Iowa.
*Krapfel, J. W................................Waterloo, Iowa.
*Lounsberry, J. G., Corporal..................Union, Iowa.
*Morgan, Arie.................................Greeley, Iowa.
McCartney, Charles P..........................Topeka, Kansas.
Owens, A......................................Castalia, Iowa.
Palmer, Silas N., Commissary..................Vermillion, D. T.

Pocock, C...Lake City, Iowa.
Rudolph, Arthur F..Canton, D. T.
Ranslow, George P..Minneapolis, Minn.
*Schoonover, L., Corporal...Anamosa, Iowa.
*Scott, D. W...Wheatland, Iowa.
Scott, Wiley..Tipton, Iowa.
Schener, Louis...Minneapolis, Minn.
Skinner, E. J...Manchester, Iowa.
*Skinner, Benjamin F...Manchester, Iowa.
Shaver, Joseph ....Eldora, Iowa.
Severance, F. H..Grundy Center, Iowa.
Soule, J...Wahoo, Neb.
*Stone, James L...Delhi, Iowa.
Trene, S. W...Manchester, Iowa.
Thompson, S. B...Grundy Center, Iowa.
*Trenchard, S. W..Manchester, Iowa.
Wells, E. L...Wallace, Kansas.
Walker, George W...Grundy Center, Iowa.
Young, John M..Oskaloosa, Iowa.

COMPANY H.

Westcott, Riley, Captain..Juniata, Neb.
McCormick, A. U., Captain...Chariton, Iowa.
Craig, Samuel T., Lieutenant..Albia, Iowa.
Mark, George, M., Lieutenant..Desoto, Iowa.
Allen, J. C..Superior, Neb.
Bates, Joseph L..Bethlehem, Iowa.
Bernard, Washington..Melrose, Iowa.
Cranse, Stephen..Leon, Iowa.
Craig, James...Marysville, Iowa.
*Cowan, William H..Flaglers, Iowa.
Carlton, L. B..Albia, Iowa.
*Carroll, N. A...Melrose, Iowa.
Calahan, C. W..Chariton, Iowa.
Dull, Thomas H...Albia, Iowa.
Elder, D. M..Augusta, Kansas.
Ferman, James H..Red Cloud, Neb.
Ferman, D. H...Wilber, Neb.
French, A. H...Superior, Neb.
Foley, L. M..Hampton, Neb.
Fautz, Thomas F..Albia, Iowa.
Gilbert, Nathan..Russell, Iowa.
Gilbert, John..Melrose, Iowa.
Grey, Thomas...New London, Iowa.
10

Gray, T. C..Smith Center, Kansas.
*Hodges, David...Ottumwa, Iowa.
Harrington, Ozra ....Elk City, Kansas.
Hall, Joseph L..Chariton, Iowa.
Hampton, John..Suteon, Neb.
Hampton, John..Fairmont, Neb.
Jones, Isaac S...Albia, Iowa.
Jefferson, M. M..Linnville, Iowa.
Kenworthy, D. C...Georgetown, Iowa.
Kester, S. M..Albia, Iowa.
Kessdall, Thomas..Galveston, Texas.
Lynch, J. F..Marina, Iowa.
Lafollette, Adam...Russell, Iowa.
Miller, Henry M...Chariton, Iowa.
Mark, James M...Desoto, Iowa.
Mank, John M..Chariton, Iowa.
Matson, John B...Austin, Texas.
Maxwell, W. T...Creston, Iowa.
McDowell, John..Ellenwood, Kansas.
McCoy, Moses S..Melrose, Iowa.
Neill, Dyas...Clio, Iowa.
Neil, Henry...Clio, Iowa.
Newell, G. W...Muscatah, Kansas.
Parmenter, W. O..Chariton, Iowa.
Rhoades, J. B...Chariton, Iowa.
Reitzell, Blair...Hopeville, Iowa.
Snook, J. N...Chariton, Iowa.
Snook, William...Weldon, Iowa.
Sinclair, Robert...Clio, Iowa.
Spurgin, William, H..Panora, Iowa.
Smith, A. J..Alexandria, Neb.
Staggers, Joseph, L...Creston, Iowa.
Sullivan, M. W...Melrose, Iowa.
Shepherd, J. H...Soldier City, Kansas.
Teas, Joseph B...Chariton, Iowa.
Thompson, George C.......................................Clio, Iowa.
Wells, Sidney...Chariton, Iowa.
*Webster, D. K...Fern Prairie, W. T.
Wilson, C. C..Chariton, Iowa.

COMPANY I.

*Dinsmore, D. C., Captain................................Kirkville, Iowa.
Dilley, Amos, Captain.....................................Adel, Iowa.
Springer, J. H., Lieutenant................................Carlton, Neb.

Kitterman, William A., Lieutenant..................Kirkville, Iowa.
Bishop, William ....Ottumwa, Iowa.
Bickley, Thomas...Ottumwa, Iowa.
Briles, Noah W..Neosho, Kansas.
Bottorff, W..Richland, Iowa.
Braden, John L...Ioka, Iowa.
Bollin, G...Nauvoo, Ills.
Caldwell, Robert P......................................Ottumwa, Iowa.
*Crocker, B. F...Martinsburg, Iowa.
Chapman, A. J...Tuskeega, Iowa.
Dodge, J. E..Long Island, Kansas.
Dickens, G. W..Competine, Kansas.
*Donnell, Samuel H.....................................Martinsburg, Iowa.
*Donnell, Oliver H......................................Martinsburg, Iowa.
*Donnell, Robert L......................................Sigourney, Iowa.
*Daly, Frank..Pontoosic, Ills.
Dodge, J. D...Prairie View, Kansas.
Earle, William D..Decatur, Iowa.
England, James R. P.....................................Bloomfield, Iowa.
Godfrey, Harrison..Ottumwa, Iowa.
Horton, Tyrus..Martinsburg, Iowa.
*Hawk, Ezra..Martinsburg, Iowa.
Hoyne, Samuel R...Martinsburg, Iowa.
Hollingsworth, A...Abington, Iowa.
Hollingsworth, B...Nevada, Iowa.
Harlan, Henry C...Nauvoo, Ills.
Hampton, James I..Piketon, Mo.
Hawk, Washington.......................................Beaver City, Neb.
Jusher, Andrew...Lucas, Iowa.
*Johnson, A. J..Martinsburg, Iowa,
Jacobs, James W...Sigourney, Iowa.
Kempton, Seth T..Hopkins, Mo.
Kenyen, G. W...Loveland, Colo.
Lynn, H. C...Martinsburg, Iowa.
Leach, J. J...Pittsburgh, Kansas.
*McAuley, William......................................Pontoosic, Ill.
Meyers, T. J..Burlington, Iowa.
Mallonee, U. A...Ottumwa, Iowa.
Mallonee, William D.....................................Martinsburg, Iowa.
Patterson, T. E...Anamosa, Iowa.
Parish, A...Schuyler, Neb.
*Phelps, A. B..Competine, Kansas.
Phelps, James H..Abingdon, Iowa.
Parish, Alonzo..Ridgly, Neb.
Priest, George W...Eldon, Iowa.
Raser, Martin...Eagle Pass, Texas.
Reily, William H...Oskaloosa, Iowa.

Shreeve, John...Ottumwa, Iowa.
*Sylvester, George W...Highland Center, Kas.
Streete, William C...Martinsburg, Iowa.
Smith, Thomas T ....Eagle Pass, Texas.
*Thompson, E. C................... ....Agency City.
Van Hoosen, William...Beaver City, Neb.
*Walker, Samuel C...Batavia, Kansas.
Williams, Conrad................ ....Competine, Kansas.

COMPANY K.

Freeman, R. L., Captain.......................................San Francisco, Cal.
Russell, John M., Captain.....................................Mill Run, Pa.
Barnes, Thomas H., Captain................................Waukon, Iowa.
Keeler, Charles F., Lieutenant............................Chicago, Ills.
Carpenter, W. W., Lieutenant..............................Fairfax, Vermont.
Sowles, H. H., Lieutenant.....................................Keota, Iowa.
Adams, Nick..Elkader, Iowa.
*Atwood, C. P..Anamosa, Iowa.
Baker, John T.... ....Decorah, Iowa.
Baldwin, Moses..Castalia, Iowa.
Border, John..McGregor, Iowa
*Bowman, T. B..Green, Iowa.
*Bricker, E..Wilton, Iowa.
Douglas, John H..Sibley, Iowa
Esty, Wilber..Tama, Iowa.
*Fitzsimons, John, Corporal................................Monticello, Iowa.
Farris, Royal P..Downs, Kansas.
Fairchild, A. H..Meridan, Conn.
Green, Melvin...Castalia, Iowa.
Harmon, Edward..Des Moines, Iowa.
Howouth, John L..Monona, Iowa.
Heman, Henry L...
*Herriman, W. B...Wadena, Iowa.
Kinsley, Jason W...North McGregor, Iowa.
Kelley, John B..West Point, Ills.
*Jones Allen..Buffalo, Iowa.
*Lyons, J. A..Guthrie Center, Iowa.
McClosky, Alex...Decorah, Iowa.
Oswald, D. C..Denver, Col.
Oathout, George..Luana, Iowa.
Orcutt, Vincent..Hot Springs, Ark.
Pease, Frank...Silver City, Ark.
Phillips, O. A...Volga City, Iowa.
*Phelon, James, Farrier......................................Anamosa, Iowa.
Reid, Lewis..Waukon, Iowa.

Reynolds, Edward..St. Olaf, Iowa.
Robey, Colins...Rossville, Iowa.
Scott, George S..Little Rock, Ark.
Sherp, Allen..Castalia, Iowa.
Stillians, Samuel...Hardin, Iowa.
*Swingle, N. M...Muscatine, Iowa.
Shelhamer, Jesse..Elkader, Iowa.
Tupper, Thomas...Luana, Iowa.
Virden, Lewis...Mt. Pleasant, Iowa.

COMPANY L.

McIntyre, D. C., Captain..Arkansas City, Ark.
Simeral, James M., Captain......................................Omaha, Neb.
Anderson, J. L...Schuyler, Neb.
Arault, James P...Quasqueton, Iowa.
Brown, J. V..Georgetown, Colo.
*Bunn Caleb...Cherokee, Iowa.
Barnes, Alexander...Salem, Kansas.
Blair, T. F...Quasqueton, Iowa.
Brunson, Andrew...Quasqueton, Iowa.
Brulot, August..Dubuque, Iowa.
*Chase, C. A..Rochester, N. Y.
Davis, James...Cascade, Iowa.
*Esson, C. G...Dubuque, Iowa.
*Foote, W. W...Dubuque, Iowa.
Grinder, Peter..Dubuque, Iowa.
*Guthrie, William...Golden, Iowa.
Hardin, S. W..Falls City, Iowa.
Hitchens, John..Hazleton, Iowa.
Hughes, D. H..Waterloo, Iowa.
*Jordan, M. V...Lettsville, Iowa.
*La Franc, Louis..Dubuque, Iowa.
Leonard, H. J...Beloit, Wis.
Lillie, M. B...Lost Nation, Iowa.
*Maurice, Nicholas...Monticello, Iowa.
*Miller, Andrew..Manchester, Iowa.
Miller, William..Winthrop, Iowa.
Mallory, Warren..Winthrop, Iowa.
Merrill, R...Hazelton, Iowa.
*Miller, C. E., Sergeant.......................................Severance, Kansas.
*Marnwaring, L. B..Wheatland, Iowa.
*Mead, H. H..Dubuque Iowa.
McKillop, D. C...Seward, Neb.
Newell, Charles..Quasqueton, Iowa.
Rice, J. E...Deadwood, D. T.
Swartzel, Davis..Quasqueton, Iowa.
Somers, Joab...Portland, Ind.

11

Seward, Joshua...St. Joseph, Mo.
Slade, C. M...Lincoln, Neb.
Slade, William...Nauvoo, Ills.
Stenger, Joseph..Seapo, Kansas.
Turner, George P..Quasqueton, Iowa.
*Thomas, A. B...Ames, Iowa.
Welliver, N. W..McGregor, Iowa.
Walton, A. E..Grenola, Kansas.
Wallace, William..Quasqueton, Iowa.
*Wise, John..Bellevue, Iowa.

COMPANY M.

Townsend, Sol., Captain..Pleasanton, Kansas.
Crosby, James, P., Captain..Black R Falls, Wis
Allen, George..Castalia, Iowa.
Bronson, D. W. C...Camanche, Iowa.
Boone, Noah..Clinton, Iowa.
Burke, P. H..Victor, Iowa.
Bennington, George...Decorah, Iowa.
Bates, Joseph L..Bethlehem, Iowa.
Barr, Peter..Clinton, Iowa.
*Boyd, Joseph..Davenport, Iowa.
Ballard, N. W...Mt. Vernon, Iowa.
Ballard, M...Fulton, Neb.
Covey, Samuel C..Lyons, Iowa.
Cummings, W. M...Independence, Iowa.
Clappen, H...Dysart, Iowa.
Dean, L. E...Lyons, Iowa.
*Darwin, A. A..Lyons, Iowa.
Dean Daniel..Lyons, Iowa.
*Direst, Hans..Lyons, Iowa.
Deerham, Ed..Hampton, Iowa.
Davidson, W. H...Quincy, Ills.
Decker, James..Edgington, Ills.
Dean, Miram..Castalia, Iowa.
Dutcher, C. L..Decatur, Texas.
Davy, F. A...Morrison, Colo.
Emin, Rid..Tomison, Ills.
Eleo, Thomas C...Parker, Dak.
*Grandy, John..Nora Springs, Iowa.
*Gaston, A. D., Quarter Master's Sergeant...................................Ames, Iowa.
Gordon, Nathan...Burlington, Iowa.
Green, Melville..Castalia, Iowa.
Hunting, W. H..Clinton, Iowa.
Hoffman, Rudolph...Lyons, Iowa.
Harrad, Hans...South Warsaw, Ohio.
*Hathaway, W. W..Davenport, Iowa.

Hoops, John M..Dallas, Iowa.
Harris, Silas W..Lime Springs, Iowa.
Hills, W. W., Corporal..Valley City, Iowa.
Holtz, Nicholas..Charlotte, Iowa.
Jordon, Martin..Lyons, Iowa.
*Kilmer, J........... ....Camanche, Iowa.
Lillis, M. D..Clinton, Iowa.
Lewis, George..Grenola, Kansas.
*Mackinson, John W..Calhoun, Mo.
McDowell, West...Morrison, Iowa.
Mathews, W. H...New Providence, Tenn.
Miner, R. E..Thompson, Ills.
Miller, William..Independence, Iowa.
McMartin, Peter ....Castalia, Iowa.
Mullen, E. J...Hayes City, Kansas.
Nettle, George T...Perry, Iowa.
Osgood, Charles J...Valley Falls, Kansas.
Quinn, Peter..Traer, Iowa.
*Rigby, W. H...Stanwood, Iowa.
Rice, George W ....Mt. Vernon, Iowa.
Ruff, Sol ....Cedar Rapids, Iowa.
Stamper, Joseph...Moberly, Mo.
Slosburg, John ....Lincoln, Iowa.
*Stuhr, John...Rock Island, Ills.
Sprague, J. W...Laporte, Iowa.
Sears, George ....Onslow, Iowa.
Stonman, Louis...Denison City, Texas.
Stoops, Henry J..Independence, Iowa.
Stoops, George W...Independence, Iowa.
*Tierray, John, H..Clinton, Iowa.
Tietzgens, J. H..Chariton, Mo.
Thompson, George...Mt. Vernon, Iowa.
Varley, Martin..Oskaloosa, Iowa.
*Wirth, Joseph...Angus, Iowa.
*Wilkes, T. R..Cedar Bluffs, Kansas,
Williams, David..Kansas City, Mo.
Wise, James H..Clinton, Iowa.
Walling, W. J..Leigh, Neb.
White, John..Moline, Ills.
Walker, George W...Grundy Center, Iowa.
Wilson, John...Traer, Iowa.
Wall, Edward...Clinton, Iowa.

www.ingramcontent.com/pod-product-compliance
Lightning Source LLC
Chambersburg PA
CBHW021518090426
42739CB00007B/669